THE LOST
SOPHOCLES

Akiko Kiso

VANTAGE PRESS
New York / Washington / Atlanta
Los Angeles / Chicago

Copyright © 1984 by Akiko Kiso

Published by Vantage Press, Inc.
516 West 34th Street, New York, New York 10001

Manufactured in the United States of America
ISBN: 533-05903-8

Library of Congress Catalog Card No.:83-90886

Contents

Preface

My title may sound ambitious, but I am not offering a thorough study of the fragments of Sophocles, nor am I proposing an entirely new interpretation of his works. The five chapters that follow attempt something much more modest; I shall merely try to suggest a perspective in which the seven preserved plays may be reviewed.

Sophocles wrote more than ten times that number of plays; from the lost majority, the surviving fragments are hopelessly meager. In the case of Euripides, who was the most popular of the three great tragedians in the acting tradition and with reading public of the later centuries, the remnants are so plentiful and of such good quality that scholars have elicited a great deal that could not have been learned by studying the extant plays alone. Far less can be deduced from the lost plays of Sophocles, and the paucity of material has not encouraged critics to explore it.

Moreover, the remarkable similarity of these fully preserved plays to each other is problematical. How closely does one resemble another? There are differences of theme and of historical context; the state of the author's maturity is another differentiating factor. We can, however, readily identify half a dozen characteristics common to all seven plays. The principal character of each presents certain features and preoccupations that can be summed up in a few key words.

Meanwhile, there is a widely accepted view since the nineteenth century that the seven plays were "selected" for use in schools. If that was what actually happened, we can assume a certain intention, perhaps educational, to account for the question of why these seven plays, all of a similar kind, survived and not others. Whatever the history was, the fact remains that our extant Sophocles is marked with outstanding homogeneity; his heroes and heroines, from first to last, show a remarkable kinship. One result of this is that Sophoclean tragedy can easily be categorized rather too neatly. Until 1950, the critics took the simple view that his plays were like sermons, exhorting the spectator toward piety and *sophrosyne* (self-restraint). The dramatist was regarded as a symbol of "classicism" in all its harmony and serenity.

Then C. Whitman published his book *Sophocles: a Study of Heroic Humanism* (Cambridge, Mass., 1951), opening the eyes of his readers to the tragic heroism that the leading characters of Sophoclean drama display. The high value that Sophocles places on their lofty morality is now widely accepted as the most typical feature of his tragedy. Their idealistic standards are contrasted with the worldly wisdom of "the little people who wish to be safe."

The antithesis has been elucidated and emphasized by other scholars, and especially in the vigorous and eloquent writings of B. M. W. Knox (*The Heroic Temper: Studies in Sophoclean Tragedy* (Berkeley and London, 1964) and others). Now, however, the danger exists of simplification in the other direction, because these high-minded heroes have such a strong appeal to the audience; the image of the noble, uncompromising Sophoclean hero, defying all the values and authorities he cannot accept and persisting in his decision even at the cost of his own life, becomes too dominant and threatens to dispel less salient but nevertheless significant qualities. It begins to be schematized, even to the exclusion of unobtrusive characteristics. Portrayal of the traits incongruent with the simple stereotyped formula is discouraged, refused, even attacked as detracting from and injuring the greatness of the poet. The situation can deteriorate so far as to allow deification, and nothing makes a writer more difficult to understand.

My only excuse for writing, when so much excellent interpretation and criticism has already been published to improve our appreciation of Sophocles' dramatic poetry, must be that the greatness of Sophocles seems to be peculiarly in need of defence against those who think, with confident disregard for the ill-documented area of Sophocles' literature, that the existing plays are sufficient testimony to his creative genius. I have no doubt that the extant drama of Sophocles is a precious heritage passed down to us, the whole of mankind, to share with wonder and admiration. But Sophocles had a wider interest, greater capacity, and richer accomplishments than the surviving plays attest to.

The difficulties of producing a coherent and substantial book on the subject of lost plays and fragments are all too obvious. I am well aware that a mere fragment, taken out of context, may mislead. Even the successful reconstruction of a play (if that is possible) can only provide a mere skeleton. It may give us some idea of the plot or allow us to guess at some of the characters, but we cannot expect the actual play to come to life before us. The most a laborious study can offer is only a hypothesis consistent with the evidence available to us.

Nevertheless, immensely handicapped as we are, one can still propose something worth considering. By carefully examining the fragments that are substantial, one can fill a real gap, which studies only of the extant plays have failed to do. One can regain the faded figures of some of the characters who have been eclipsed by the towering grandeur of the surviving heroes. We have inherited no small number of such attempts, many of them enlightening our ignorance or rectifying our wrong assumptions about the poet. If this little book should follow them and reveal only a few aspects of Sophocles hidden behind the "orthodox" picture of the poet, my attempt will not have been made in vain.

The plan of my book will be that I start with the poet's earliest preserved play, *Ajax*; in chapter 1 I shall make use of some recently discovered fragments, trying to show how the tragic heroism of Sophocles can be more thoroughly appreciated when reviewed within the context of related fragmentary plays. This will enable us to affirm the basic validity of the "orthodox" view of Sophoclean drama and also to acquire a perspective that approaches only via the fully preserved plays may have lacked.

In chapter 2 and chapter 3, I shall dwell on the glimpses we can get of two of the lost plays. I shall examine afresh papyrus and book fragments, scholarly references, and recounted versions of later writers. I shall try to establish dramatic time and place, the cast of the characters, and the probable sequence of the action. The choice of the lost plays is subject to the quality as well as to the quantity of their remnants, for we must avoid idle speculations based on insecure foundation. Consequently, I have felt obliged to confine myself to a discussion of only those two lost plays in which the hidden face of the poet seems to loom more discernibly than in the less fortunate remains of Sophoclean literature, and which are not without bearings on the main points of my concern. Any reconstruction of a lost play must be of the most tentative sort. But if such attempts in full-scale reconstruction of chosen lost plays should help us to reconsider the already known aspects of Sophocles in his search for tragic heroism and thus lead us to a deeper understanding of the beauty and power of his poetic drama, these chapters will not have been worthless.

In chapter 4, I shall return to one of the poet's latest extant plays, *Philoctetes*. After a survey of some of the neglected areas of Sophoclean dramatic art, we shall be able, I hope, to reexamine the play with less philological preoccupation. Since the play is dominated by the hero, no less typically "Sophoclean" than those of the other extant plays, our discussion will inevitably be on the tragic heroism of Sophocles. But I shall adopt a viewpoint almost opposite to the "orthodox" one.

The arrangement of the chapters does not necessarily indicate chronological order of the plays, except that the development of Sophocles' work, which obviously is there between the two extant plays I have put in the beginning and closing chapters of my inquiry, may have included such aspects as suggested by the two lost plays placed in between. I shall make some additional remarks in chapter 5, which, however, must be limited to a few selected topics, because the hypotheses presented in the preceding chapters vary in their degree of availability for further discussion.

My book is addressed primarily to those who are already familiar with the extant plays. Yet readers less well grounded in the classics are by no means to be discouraged; nearly all the Greek quotations have been translated or paraphrased. What I will say owes much to and shares many details with the works of earlier critics and living scholars. I have had to confine myself to acknowledging them only in passing, lest the reader's attention be detracted. There are many points of reference of which I have not mentioned the origin, but without these valuable works of earlier scholarship, I should have been unable to compose this book.

Among those to whom I owe personal debts, I must put first Professor Chiaki Matsudaira and the late Professor T. B. L. Webster. I owe more than I am aware to the Institute of Classical Studies: to Professor R. P. Winnington-Ingram, former director, to Professor E. W. Handley, director, to Miss A. Totolos, the secretary, to Miss M. M. Packer, assistant to the secretary, to Mr. J. M. Murphy, assistant editor, who has kindly edited and corrected my English style, and to other members of the staff. I am grateful for criticism and encouragement during the years of my study in Great Britain and in Japan to Mrs. P. E. Easterling. I also owe thanks to Professor W. H. Willis for his generous help when an earlier version of chapter 2 appeared in *Greek, Roman and Byzantine Studies*. By the kind permission of its editors, the article is reprinted here. Chapter 3 is a revised form of a paper read at a Greek-Latin drama discussion meeting jointly held by the Greek Department of the University of Glasgow and the Greek Department of the University of Edinburgh. To Professor A. J. Beattie, to Professor E. K. Borthwick and the Edinburgh staff, to Professor D. M. MacDowell and the Glasgow staff, I am grateful for their great hospitality. My special thanks are due to Professor W. M. Calder III, who took the time and trouble of reading through and commenting on my manuscript. He saved me from many embarrassing errors, provided a most helpful critique, and gave me much-needed help and encouragement. His valuable suggestions improved my draft at many points. But, naturally, all mistakes and shortcomings of this book are my exclusive responsibility.

Kyoto, December 1982   *AK*

Introduction

An outstanding characteristic of the heroes of Sophocles is their self-sufficiency. They make their choices not under guidance or exhortation of the gods, not on demand or in submission to any external power, but solely as their instinct dictates. Once launched on their own voyage, they pursue it till it reaches its destination, even at the cost of an easier life. Their choice is a devotion to one idea, one wish, one thing they believe to be worthwhile, and for the sake of that choice, they have to oppose their people, their own family, fellow citizens, and comrades. They bring upon themselves suffering and destruction, since the course they have taken is not in accordance with the ordinary ways of the world. However, this enactment of the most unyielding self-assertion, of the most inexorable self-devotion, destined only to lead to ruin, attests to their greatness. By the time the play ends, the audience is fully convinced that nothing but the characters' own nature has produced that outcome, that their self-annihilation has been the only possible conclusion to their lives and that they have obtained sovereignty over the kingdom they themselves have constructed for their greatness.

If Sophocles, by creating these self-sufficient heroes, first established in Greek tragedy the idea of heroic humanism, how did he conceive and develop it, when his gods are represented, throughout his life, as reigning most powerfully and unfailingly over the vast universe and in every nook of the human world? The recognition of the indomitable divine influence that lays mortals low had been prominent in Greek thinking from the earliest days and was given one of the most penetrating literary expressions by Sophocles. All the same, the self-sufficiency of the Sophoclean hero does not yield an inch. His greatness is so invincible, so steadfast, that even the gods' interference cannot efface it; nor can any reproach or criticism by his people detract from the value of his heroism, which, though glorious and inspiring, could turn out to be destructive to society, with its too vigorous self-assertion. Oedipus gouges out his eyes, "hated by the gods" (*Oedipus Rex* 1345). Antigone goes to her tomb "mocked at by people" (*Antigone* 839). Is the Sophoclean hero accursed with permanent solitude? Is he fated to die in the face of the gods' hostility?

Since Fortune has not favored us by preserving from Sophocles more than the seven "select" plays, our search to understand his lifelong quest for tragic heroism is greatly disadvantaged. However, an examination of some remnants of the lost Sophocles, though limited in extent, may help us to see under fresh light the poet's vision of life with his thoughts on the problem of hero versus god and hero versus human society.

The Lost Sophocles

1.

Theomachy and the *Ajax*

1

Ajax is exceptional among the plays of Sophocles in that Athena appears as a dramatic character and in overt antagonism toys and trifles with the unhinged hero as she indulges in distressingly ungodlike torture. Other Sophoclean gods, verbally represented, may loom up, sometimes concretely enough, in their specific function or concern with a particular hero, and sometimes as some general absolute power or scheme, operating on its own rules yet passing from one image to another so quickly and freely that they give an impression of ubiquity or inscrutability.[1] Unlike them, the stage figure of Athena is peculiarly impressive with her callous, cruel haughtiness, that stern and hostile look, as if she were in human flesh and blood. Her merciless mockery reduces the great hero of Homeric tradition to a mutilated carcass trampled beneath the foot of a victorious enemy. Against the madness and death that this fiendish goddess sends forth, the great warrior of the Greek host is utterly helpless.

Ajax is no exception to those gigantic figures of Sophoclean tragedy, which acquire grandeur and magnificence all by themselves. It is exclusively his own intractable self that leads him to his destination. Tragedy, as always in Sophocles, begins, grows, and ends in the personality of the hero. The total impression of the play is dominated by the colossal tragic figure of Ajax.

How are we to reconcile this sublime heroism of the self-sufficient Sophoclean hero with that unusually theatrical theophany of an Olympian figure who, like the traditional deities of myths, does not fail to send forth severe punishment for her slighted honor? Is the theophany a remnant of the old style, awkwardly left in disharmony with the new Sophoclean idea of heroism?[2] The Scholiast (*Ajax* 14) remarks that the appearance of Athena is ''pleasant to the spectator.'' If it is so, what relevance does that sensory effect have to the whole of Sophoclean theater and his essential tragic heroism?

2

Athena in *Ajax Locrus* (*P. Oxy*.3151), shown in white-hot indignation at the statue of herself overturned by the Argive warriors in Troy, is as malevolent as the Athena in the extant *Ajax*. Her words on appearance, as construed by Haslam, are overbearing:[3]

> What sort of Dyras' offspring came on the
> Trojan expedition, O Argives?
> Who dared such things against gods?
> Can it be that out of the dead arose Salmoneus
> who imitated the thunders of Zeus?
> To whose [work] shall I compare this which
> dislodged the image?

The Muses in *Thamyras* are also harsh in exacting a penalty for the human arrogance of vying with divine beings in the art of musical performance. Instant blinding of the Thracian lyrist on stage (attested by Pollux's note), after a spectacular display of his marvelous talent, would have impressed vividly upon the audience the vehement anger of the Muses.[4]

Another awe-inspiring figure is Apollo exhorting Artemis to shoot a Niobid daughter, suggested by W. S. Barrett's interpretation of the Oxyrhynchus papyrus fragment *P. Oxy*.2805.[5] Barrett found connected sequences preceding and following this scene in the fragment from Hibeh published by Grenfell and Hunt in 1897 (and 1906)[6] and attributed to Sophocles' *Niobe* by Blass in 1897.[7] Neither Blass' identification of the Hibeh papyrus nor Barrett's of *P. Oxy.*2805 is based on any external evidence to prove the ascription to Sophocles' *Niobe*. But both have such indisputably precise correspondences of circumstantial evidence (which is thoroughly discussed in Barrett's contribution to Carden's *Papyrus Fragments of Sophocles*; see note 5) that no authorship other than Sophocles' can be inferred. No argument has so far counterattacked the proposition, nor will any be able to, I believe, in the future. Radt has printed both, though with asterisks, in his 1977 edition of *Fragmenta Sophoclis*.[8] Other critics have agreed.[9] The appearance of the gods in the midst of the action in a Sophoclean play, which was previously doubted, is, now that the Athena in *Ajax Locrus* is known, to be accepted as "not unprecedented."

What is the significance of these markedly theatrical strokes in Sophoclean drama? Have they any connection with, or do they offer any clue to, the question we posed about the theophany in the extant *Ajax*? All these plays with furiously exasperated god figures may be classified as theomachy (fighting against gods) in the sense that the gods become angry with men and chastise them for their presumption in thinking themselves comparable to the gods in strength, beauty, and so on.

Homer knew that kind of myth. His heroes are heedful of divine superiority and talk of the wide gap between divine and human existence, which denies great prosperity and undiluted happiness to men.[10] But in view of the very strict limits set to man's hope of eternal felicity, human beings are on most intimate terms with gods. Homeric heroes are gods' favorites and sons. Achilles' glory is blessed, and care is lavished upon him by Thetis; Agamemnon's dignity is not diminished but increased by that of Zeus; Hector's or Sarpedon's valour is pitied by Zeus. The actual appearances of the gods in the heroes' moments of prowess account for the human trust in divine affection and the awareness of the mortals of their dependence upon the gods'

3

grace. In the *Odyssey*, Athena praises Odysseus' cunning in an almost doting tone, as if she, like Narcissus, is looking at her own reflection (13.287ff). Two references to theomachy in the *Iliad* (5.407ff, 6.138ff) are both incidental.

It has been observed that the old idea of human limitation versus transcending divine power and wisdom meets a new emotional reaction in the Archaic Age.[11] Growing population needed colonization overseas, involved class struggle and economic tension, and allowed new thoughts, religious, philosophical, scientific, and so on, to flood out. The Archaic Age is usually regarded as a time of political and social cataclysm. It deepens the general feeling of human insecurity that, though prominent in Homer, did not necessarily result in a sense of harsh antagonism between mortals and immortals or a notion of the gods' resentment against or jealousy of human elevation and success. But the deploration of ruined peers, discontent of the oppressed, and anguish of the wandering colonists, when they are reflected upon and voiced as the painful laments for human helplessness and the futility of human purpose, may assume a tone of religious fear and apprehension, and one may suspect in the stern look of the world the gods' ill will, even malice or vindictive feelings against human prosperity. One may discern already in the passionate lamentation of Archilochus, Alcman, Theognis, Semonides, and other lyric poets of the Archaic Age, expressed in varying shades and forms of pessimism, an air of anxiety about divine jealousy (*phthonos*).[12] No matter what success, what happiness, human beings may obtain, they are incessantly jeopardized by the watchful eyes of divine beings. For the benignant patrons and patronesses of the heroes no longer rejoice in bestowing profuse grace on their human favorites, as they did in Homeric epic, but bear a grudge and punish, when the ephemeral creatures prosper and thrive. The conception may become conspicuous in one or the other of the early classical writings, and we find in Herodotus an almost obsessive sense of awe and apprehension of divine revenge.[13]

The brief survey of the difference between the Homeric and the later sentiments on human limitations, or rather of the continuity all the way from Homer through the Archaic Age down to the early classical writers in their appreciation of the deep gulf between god and man may be supplemented by a few words on moral concern on the part of the human beings. The recognition of human infirmity by post-Homeric poets calls at the same time for a corresponding endeavor to impose human moral standards not only on the individual but also on society at large. Hesiod's stress on honest labour, due measure as the strongest shield against the crushing powers of external conditions of life, is noticeably saturated with a consciousness of social justice.[14] Solon warned against every kind of excess. His zeal for the "middle road" was fruitful in political reforms and offered a guiding principle for *polis*-states.[15]

The tragic drama that came after the excitement of the Archaic Age, along with the era of general organization, was, as a form of communal as well as religious experience, a suitable medium by means of which the fragile human condition, with all its complexities, was to be thoroughly studied, and it is in the tragic poets that we see the first flowering of the literary expression of theomachy.

Aeschylus busied himself in searching for a religious and moral system from a sense of despair over human instability. The arbitrary powers that are felt to interfere with human affairs are envisaged as bearers of a solemn cosmic order, with Zeus presiding over ultimate justice. An idea of submission to this divinely disposed order, that of moderation due to human limitation, is formed as a valid guide to man's conduct. For the suffering of the morally innocent, the notion of an inherited curse or deferred punishment for the guilt of their ancestors provides an explanation. It was with sufficient reason that all the extant plays of Aeschylus, in which the overstepping of human boundaries is enacted against this cosmic order, were called *theomachiae*.[16] The Danaids, in their refusal of marriage, are represented as having transgressed the limit for women, which had been decided on and supervised by Aphrodite (*Supplices* 1001ff). Xerxes is emphatically depicted as paying the penalty for violating natural law (*Persae* 742ff, 808, 827ff). Eteocles' choice is phrased as "recovering debt for Laius' sin of disobedience to the oracle" (*Septem* 745ff). Agamemnon's triumph most theatrically presented in the "carpet scene" (*Agamemnon* 958ff) occasions not only his own death but also a host of disasters and particularly Orestes' suffering. All these Aeschylean *theomachiae* are strongly accentuated by a search for theodicy and moral inquiry.

In Sophocles, the recognition of the limits, of the futility of all human achievements, and the warning against arrogance is hardly less prominent. The pessimistic vision of human infirmity against the gods' capricious power is throughout his life an essential prospect of Sophoclean drama.[17] The abysmal gloom of *Oedipus Rex* is an unparalleled example of poetic expression of that sentiment. However, in spite of the dejecting picture of man's frailty, each of his plays is dominated by the luminous grandeur of the hero. The heights of heroism reached by the principal character are insurmountable. How can this impression of human greatness be created while the hero's situation in god-man relationship remains utterly helpless?

If we look closer into Sophocles' representation of the story of Niobe in comparison to Aeschylus', it will be clear that Sophocles found a way to reach the idea of tragic heroism by making a notably aesthetic approach in the dramatization of theomachy, while Aeschylus, paying as much attention to theatrical effect,[18] was essentially concerned with the religious and moral aspects of the myths.

The story of Niobe, a Lydian, daughter of Tantalus, married to Amphion, king of Thebes, had been well known since olden times.[19] Having seven sons and seven daughters[20] (in Sophocles, Aeschylus' number is unknown), she boasted of her superiority over Leto, who had only two. The angry goddess let her children massacre all Niobe's. The mourning mother turned into an ever-weeping rock.

It is a plausible guess that Aeschylus' *Niobe* could have shown how calamity fell on the consecutive generations of the insolent Tantalids in a grand-scale trilogy,[21] but, as far as we can be sure from the fragments and other testimonia,[22] Aeschylus started the action of the *Niobe* three days after the deaths of her children.[23] Niobe was placed on the tomb of her children silent and sitting immovable for a considerable part of the play.[24] During that time, the Chorus "rattled off a string of lyrics" (Ar., *Ran.* 914–15). Tantalus came to mourn and to fetch Niobe back to Lydia (Fr.273M, 10–11). Some other person (perhaps Antiope, Niobe's mother-in-law[25]) appeared onstage to lament (Fr.273M). The play resembles *Persae* in dramatic handling of theomachic material in that the actual deed of *hybris* (boasting) and the divine indignation is put outside the action. Repentant remarks and lamentation for the *hybris* that has been punished would have occupied a great part of the action. What else could be sung about with "(a string of) four lyric odes, sung one after the other" (Ar., *Ran* 914–15) in *Niobe*, during the long silence of the heroine, than the heavenly blow that had visited one member of an accursed family of hereditary arrogance? When the speaker of Fr.273M says, "the god first creates a fault in man, when he wants to put a family down root and branch" (15), the deed of *hybris* is remorsefully recollected. We find a similar moral anguish in the bitter regrets of Darius in *Persae* 743. A grave sense of guilt sustains the atmosphere of religious fear and apprehension. Prestige itself is pregnant with evil and is imperilled by the inevitability of an imminent divine blow. The wealthy and the powerful in Aeschylus are always menaced by an overhanging cloud of misfortune.[26] When the prosperity and luxury of Persian royalty are described (*Pers.* 1–154), an ominous sense of impending calamity is felt. Aeschylus' concern in dealing with a typically thoemachic subject seems to have its origin in the ide-

7

ological aspect of the god-man relationship. He is preoccupied with the thought of *hybris* calling forth *ate* (calamity), of justice operating in the dispensations of the gods.[27] We should be justified in expecting his *Niobe* to be a play where *ate* is discussed exhaustively from the viewpoint of theodicy and human ethics in an attitude of dread and religious reverence.

The Sophoclean approach to the story is remarkably different. He laid out before the spectators the very battle of divine and human competitors. According to Barrett's brilliant reconstruction, Apollo, from above the palace roof looking down behind the stage-building as if into the inner courtyard of the palace, is pointing out to Artemis that the second and the third (or the third and the fourth) Niobid daughters are engaged in some ordinary household work. The unsuspecting girls are easy prey for Artemis' archery (P. Grenf. II 6(a) fr.4 = 445R). In the succeeding scene, to which Barrett assigns *P. Oxy.*2805 (see Carden, *Fragments*, 198 with n. 61), another girl (the fourth or the fifth) is detected by Apollo cowering in terror, taking refuge by the bins in a storeroom. The girl must by now have noticed what is happening to her sisters. Apollo's words:

> Do you see that frightened one in the house? The one who is cowering alone secretly in the tun-store and by the bins?
> Are you not going to despatch a swift arrow at her before she hides herself?

In another fragment from Hibeh (P. Grenf. II 6(a) fr.1 = 442R), one still-surviving girl is heard begging the goddess not to kill her (behind the stage, according to Barrett):

> . . . I pray, mistress!
> [Please, do not] shoot nor kill me!

The scenes here revealed are doubtless from the sequence of consecutive murders of the Niobid daughters by Artemis. It seems that Sophocles made the slaughter of the girls, which would normally be narrated by someone in Greek tragedy as it was happening inside the palace, a visual stage representation with divine and human characters together in action. He brought at least one Niobid daugher on to stage[28] in all the charm of childhood (P. Grenf. II 6(a) fr.3 = 444R, 5–7). Plutarch's quotation offers evidence that the deaths of the adolescent sons were described in loving detail (*Amat.* 17 760—calling on a lover with one's last breath = 448R, also P. Grenf. II 6(a) fr.2 = 443R).[29] Apollo and Artemis, Leto's pride, also appear in the full bloom of their youthful beauty, and the virgin goddess shows her graceful but ruthless art of archery. The confrontation of the children is the highlight of the strife of two proud mothers.

Such theatrical ostentation of human beauty, man's claim and aspiration glorified by the opposing divine emulation, can atone for what is essentially wretched in the human condition in the god-man relationship. For the Greek gods, molded after human models, their physical appearances contoured in the shape of men and women, their personalities built up from human nature, their roles and skills differentiated as in human life,[30] are nothing but beautiful men and women, and divine envy, occasioned only when the gods feel their own superiority imperilled by human elevation, enhances the brilliance of human aspiration and attainments.

Ascription to the gods not only of a human figure and temper, but also of human endowments such as fecundity, martial prowess, physical attractiveness, manual skill, and so on, attests to man's pride and confidence in these possessions, and human existence as a lively combination of these assets is something to be admired. This is illustrated most characteristically by the anthropomorphism of the Homeric gods, how they can serve as an offset to the grace and beauty of the Homeric heroes and heroines.[31] Sophocles, the best disciple of Homer (*Vita* 20), would have seen this artistic appeal of the anthropomorphism of the Homeric gods and demonstrated most pointedly in scenes of direct confrontation of divine and human contestants in stories of theo-machy.

When these harsh but elegant Olympian figures manifest themselves on Sophoclean stage as attested by the scanty frag-ments where there is evidence of the actual presence of the gods, their celestial illumination brightens up the poor ephemeral op-ponents and the tight tension of rivalry magnifies their stature. Moreover, a picture of a proud man's sudden downfall, when cast into relief against immortality, is doubly gratifying to the viewers' aesthetic sensibility. For no mortal beauty can be more pathetically and touchingly felt than in its concurrent moment of success and ruin. The more agilely Apollo moves about and the more swiftly Artemis emits unfeeling arrows to exterminate in-nocent Niobids, the more plainly divine superiority is accentuated in patent contrast to human infirmity. However, the spectators are simultaneously treated to a scene where Niobe's happiness in her possession of so many children is given the last but most resplendent radiation, the youngest (or one of the youngest) of the daughters, a special delight and prize to a mother, appearing before their eyes in the utmost grace and sweetness of her girl-hood.

Let us remember that in *Thamyras,* before the musician was struck blind, his fabulous art of lyre performance was actually displayed on stage (*Vita* 4, Athen., 1.20f, also see note 4), which, played by the poet himself, made so entrancing a tableau as to be immortalized by Polygnotus on the wall of Stoa Poikile (Paus., 9. 30.2).[32] A fragment suggests that Thamyras proudly chanted his illustrious pedigree (Fr.242R).[33] His sudden punishment with blindness and loss of his musical skill would have been strikingly effective as a reminder of the highest attainment and happiness. Scenes of ruthless divine retaliation upon human beings who make extreme claims for a specific human asset—Thamyras, the lyrist, Niobe, the proud mother—are thus one condensed expres-sion of the rich sensibility of the Greek dramatic poetry, which, with its strong concrete imagination, sees men in their most beautiful and exalted forms in the splendor of heavenly light.[34]

The scene cited above from the *Ajax Locrus* also suggests sheer human weakness faced with divine intervention. The play unquestionably treated the incident summarized by Proclus from the *Iliu Persis*: "Ajax, son of Oileus, by force tearing away Cassandra, upturns Athena's wooden statue. Angry because of this the Greeks want to punish Ajax by stoning. But he flees to the altar of Athena and is saved from the imminent danger."[35] Athena's anger is presupposed in the *Odyssey* (3.135 and 3.145), and Ajax's ultimate death after the second sin of boasting, together with the deaths of other Greeks, is recorded in the *Odyssey* (4.502, 5.108ff).[36] No other episode of the Locrian Ajax is preserved. "The rape of Cassandra" had been a familiar theme in art and literature since Archaic times.[37]

The plan of the play is so obscure that nothing can be inferred plausibly except that Ajax survives Athena's anger (Lucianus, *De salt.* 46).[38] It is reasonably conjectured by critics that a court of law was held to decide Ajax's case by the Greek generals, but that Ajax managed to escape the capital penalty.[39] Pearson speculated that his oath to the court was a perjury;[40] Robert, that he promised atonement by sending from Locris two maidens to Athena's temple in Troy each year ever after.[41] Presumably because of the failure of the Greeks to punish the wrong, whatever it was, Athena arouses a storm at sea to prevent the Greek army from returning home. Ajax survives and boasts that even the gods' hostility could not beat him down. Offended by this, Poseidon throws his trident at the Gyraean rock, which the dying Ajax grasped. That the play included this incident, probably in the form of a prophecy, is undeniable.[42]

What strikes us is that Ajax, after all, is acquitted unscathed before his eventual death. Granted that he got clear away from a criminal charge by "seeking refuge at Athena's altar," he would not have been able to cope with the situation without strenuously vindicating himself against his prosecutors. Whether the eloquence of his speech saved him or not, Ajax would have presented a most-vigorous self-glorification as a distinguished warrior. What else could have been the contents of his oratory, if there was a trial scene, which seems most likely? Here would be another opportunity for unrestrained self-elevation.[43]

The death of Locrian Ajax, as told by Lucianus, is heavenly punishment. He dies utterly helpless, although proudly defiant to the end, under the gods' rage. To Ajax, the son of Telamon, death is a chosen deed of honor. To Ajax, the Judgment of the Arms, the award of Achilles' armor as the prize for bravery in which he has been judged to be inferior to Odysseus, was beyond endurance. "Ajax, becoming mad, spoils the booty of the Achaeans and kills himself."[44] The extant play *Ajax* has that suicide as its subject. We shall see what part Athena plays in the hero's drama, which marked a memorable step forward in the quest of Sophoclean tragic heroism.[45]

3

Ajax's decision for suicide is perfectly understandable in itself, since his life has become defiled with the humiliation in the Judgment of the Arms and disgrace of the slaughter of sheep. But the dramatist has taken trouble so that it appears as though Ajax's death is a punishment for his arrogance (*Aj.* 783). There is no trace of Ajax's boasting against Athena in literature earlier than Sophocles.[46] Slaughter of livestock in insanity is recorded in the Epitome of *Ilias Parva*, but without direct connection with Athena's intervention. Sophocles' introduction of Athena is, at any rate, part of his dramatic design.

But, in fact, the personal affront felt by Athena on account of Ajax's previous vaunting is hidden from the dramatic characters as well as from the audience, until when, halfway through the action, the messenger from Teucer comes and discloses Ajax's former insolence (766). What, then, is the significance of Athena's appearance to stand in opposition to an unhinged hero? If the playwright's reason was merely to explain what the madman intended to do by killing animals, he could have done this, for instance, with the words of Ajax himself after awakening from the delusion, as, in part, he does (447–56).

Athena's conversation with Ajax ends with the hero's most scornful rejection of the goddess' admonition (112–13). However, Ajax is in delusion. Delusion is another heaven-sent misfortune no less disastrous than death: man cannot do anything against it, but he can at least see himself, unmolested by objective reality, as beautiful as he wishes himself to be. Ajax, who has been stigmatized as an inferior warrior and a shameful sheep-slayer, is given in the prologue one last moment of undisturbed self-elevation. Believing himself to be rid of the dishonor, squarely facing the warrior-goddess, Ajax views himself as the greatest of the Greek soldiers and boasts himself of his martial achievements. The Athena-Ajax opposition in the prologue, therefore, not only prepares for a later moment when Ajax's haughtiness is echoed in the account of his contempt for the gods' help (768), but also visualizes the hero's pride, his excessive but beautiful claim as a renowned warrior in the traditional pattern of theomachy.

Athena, with an *aegis* or a shield and in a glittering helmet, would appear as a warrior.[47] Now that she has beaten down Ajax by inflicting an onslaught of madness on him to thwart his aim, she is the conqueror. Yet she pursues her victory, like a true warrior triumphant over the enemy, to atrocious extremes. Athena professes that this is to favour Odysseus, Ajax's mortal enemy, by assisting him on a superhuman level (66). But Odysseus is virtually outside the theomachic system, which allows special place to one singled-out individual in shoulder-to-shoulder commerce with gods. Furious animosity fills the scene of confrontation, beginning with a military term used ironically by Athena in reference to herself (συμμάχου an ally, 90).[48] Ajax's reply is condescending, even "patronizing" (91–93).[49] He is at the top of his proud feelings in his belief of having killed the Atreidae and put Odysseus under control. In an apparent mockery of Ajax's megalomaniac self-conceit, Athena insists on inquiring if he "imbrued his sword" (95). Ajax's cheerful reply that he performed "a glorious deed" (κόμπος 96)[50] gives a finishing stroke to the picture of a distinguished warrior of highest achievements. Athena gloats over the complete defeat of her enemy with derisive comments (97).

This is a combat fought in real earnest. Athena takes full advantage of the inborn weakness of her enemy. Advised to spare Odysseus a cruel whipping (111), Ajax bluntly rejects her admonition (112–13) and retorts with insulting commands to go and mind her own business (116–17). No more scornful and haughty words can come from a mortal's mouth. Ajax leaves the stage in highest spirits, quite ignorant of his own wretched situation. Athena's vindictive sporting with her victim is founded on the common rule of the military society to which Ajax adheres: be friendly to allies; be harsh to enemies.[51]

Athena's remark on Ajax after his departure is a great tribute to a defeated contestant made by the conqueror who cannot but admire his opponent's skill:

> Who was more prudent in thought, more efficient and competent in action than this man? (119–20).

The warrior-goddess showed in the battle as much martial efficiency and relentlessness as she perceived in Ajax. Equipping the confronting antagonists with mutually corresponding qualities is a technical device effective to secure artistic success in theatrical presentation of a theomachic subject. Here the actual presence of a goddess on stage in the role of a rival-warrior enables the deranged hero to acquire superhuman stature, which is his inherent quality.

When released from heaven-sent delusion, Ajax is bitterly conscious of his present position. He is, in every worldly sense, a failure, as he expressly states himself to be (393ff). He cannot bear the shame of having performed an ugly and ridiculous deed. How can he restore his honor and fame as the distinguished warrior that he believes to be his true self? Only by putting an end worthy of a hero to a dishonored life. Dramatic presentation of a self-imposed noble death can save this unfortunate hero. There are other suicides in Sophocles (more by far among his extant plays than others of the three tragedians),[52] but only Ajax's suicide is thoroughly scrutinized in the privileged position of the protagonist's deed. The four great speeches, amounting to 187 lines, shape the way for him to return to that heroic status through death. To Ajax, death is not a collapse or submission to the fate destined by a god. Although the unhappy incidents have deprived him of his prestige and share in Greek community, his belief and pride in his own virtues and nobility have not been disintegrated. He ponders and comes to be convinced that the only way to preserve them is to organize at his own discretion an honorable death worthy of his own conception of himself. He dies by throwing himself on a sword, a gift from Hector, planted in the Trojan soil. The sublime tone of the language and abundance of virile imagery of the speeches make Ajax's death the culmination of his life as a hero. No other leading character in Sophocles' extant drama is allowed such lavish expenditure of poetic luxury. Through these four speeches, Ajax becomes the master over his own death.

The particular importance of the third speech (646–92) has been repeatedly stressed by critics.[53] It is the much-disputed "deception speech." My understanding of it, after the long discussion by eminent scholars, follows the "soliloquy" view. It shows the shame-conscious warrior, yearning to "die nobly" (479),[54] now that to "live nobly" has become impossible, for the first time contemplating his own self in the perspective of time and its law of change. His identity is scrutinized in relation to the universe, where mortals are accommodated under the gods' supervision to live by the code of mutual tolerance and friendship.[55] Insecurity is indeed the fundamental condition of human existence, but its consequent demand, the criterion of concession and co-operation, is unacceptable to a man like Ajax. His pride in and conviction of distinction, that he is a hero with a hero's well-deserved privilege of holding high self-esteem, precludes any idea of conciliation. He concludes that his nature is essentially irreconcilable to this world of mutability. His only choice is to part company with human society. The death initially envisaged solely from an aesthetic viewpoint acquires ethical depth and determines his religious attitude.

The messenger's report of Calchas' words after the third speech reminds one of Athena's slighted honor. The dramatist has composed the dramatic structure in such a way that it appears, with the newly given information about Ajax's boastful remark made in the past (776), that his death has been arranged by Athena (778–79) and is bound to take place under her supervision.[56] The sense of the inevitability of a god-sent death is made more prominent since the ambiguity in Ajax's third speech has made his people rejoice in a mistaken assumption of a withdrawal from this disastrous step (695). To their eyes, death will emerge as a prewarned punishment (783) for Ajax's insolence (952), which, however, to the audience who have witnessed the scene of the hero's exaltation and then his inner fight through to a conviction of his own greatness, will have become a necessary conclusion of his own choice in remaining independent of the gods.

Ajax has not been victimized for a slip of the tongue, but has discovered himself. In the agony of the resolution of death, he creates an independent cosmos for his own greatness. He becomes successful in dying a gallant and heroic death. His last recognition of Athena's hostility is that of her obstruction to his intention of sheep-slaughter (401ff, 452).[57] In his consciousness, no divine power is working in his death. Those who feel beaten by the retaliating hand of Athena under the impending pressure of prophecy are his followers and family (952). Ajax just does not care; he has discovered himself as a mighty noble warrior (820), and his death is an acme of his life, not a breakdown. It is a departure from the divinely ordained world. Ajax pushes the divine sphere far back behind him and outgrows the traditional theomachic scheme to supercede it with a self-sufficient world of tragic heroism. Death as the result of vaunting oneself under the gods' jealous authority in the mythological formula of theomachy has here acquired a new significance crystalized in an unexcelled poetry of victory.

After *Ajax*, the great gods of the myths recede to a vague, impersonal existence far in the background behind the heroes, who will have human society to oppose in place of the gods. The dramatic demonstration of the gods' rule over the mortals becomes more and more covert and submerged, while the surface outlook of the world becomes more and more inscrutable and incomprehensible. However much the traditional gods may be appealed to, no response will come back from the remote recesses to which they have receded. The names of Olympian gods sound more and more abstract and become interchangeable. One may recognize in this aspect "a step toward symbolic interpretation of the Olympian gods."[58]

I believe traditional stories of theomachy with harsh and beautiful gods to be the cradle of Sophoclean tragic heroism. Therefore I have tried in this chapter to show the suicide of Ajax within the context of *Ajax Locrus*, *Thamyras*, and *Niobe*, heroes most likely to be struggling directly against gods within the action of the play.

The use of the theomachic pattern in creating tragic heroism is practically a matter of dramatic technique on the part of the playwright. The Sophoclean art was successful in presenting an illuminating image of Ajax's intrinsic self, when the mad hero

17

acted like a god (112–13), as if no guidance, no assistance, no interference was needed in order to be his own master. However, its significance in Sophoclean tragedy is essential. For the Sophoclean hero, as depicted in the extant plays, finishes his drama as a god in the form of a human being. Commencing with being true to his own sensibility, the hero then gives voice to his inner logic. That logic is the standard of a Sophoclean hero, too high to be accepted by ordinary people. But the hero forwards his cause throughout the action with his extraordinary strength and power and ends victorious over a world of adversities and misfortunes, in spite of his failure in terms of the ordinary ways of the world. His image as a superhuman, gigantic hero of invincible greatness is eternalized in the spectators' eyes—imperishable, not liable to change—exactly as a god. He now obtains immortality. Not only Ajax but Antigone, Oedipus in his two plays, Electra, Philocetetes, and—many would include—Heracles, if not Deianeira, all become, as it were, divine beings transcending humanity in spite of their physical deaths or misfortunes on the level of human life. Since *Ajax* is generally regarded as the earliest extant play, its hero may be taken to be the prototype with which the poet set out on his search for that heroic humanism. For we shall find this ideal of tragic heroism still alive, even more strongly, in the next-to-last extant Sophoclean drama in our discussion in chapter 4.

We may then take advantage of this typical start and advance our study, inquiring whether the poet really maintained the same notion of tragic heroism, always, in all his plays, whether or not the homogeneity of the existing plays should be attributed, say, to the fact that they form a "selection."

Ajax does not change his mind; nor do any other of the Sophoclean heroes, except Philoctetes. It is the hallmark of a Sophoclean hero that he persists in his initial decision and promotes his cause, no matter what threats or attacks may be made to break his resolve. If we come across a Sophoclean hero who changes his mind, he is worth isolating for discussion. We shall

18

meet Philoctetes in chapter 4. For the topic of chapter 2, we shall have Alcmaeon in the *Epigoni*, a famous legendary hero who, presumably, refused at first but changed his mind and killed his own mother at the command of his father, although my thesis should be confined to a very modest position, since the remainder of the original text is precious little.

2.

Alcmaeon in the *Epigoni*[1]

1

There is no recent papyrus discovery to help the reconstruction of the *Epigoni*; but a reexamination of the material that has been previously collected will allow us to draw a clearer picture of the play. The main testimonia for the myth are the following: Apollodorus, *Bibliotheca* 3.6.1, 7.2ff; Diodorus Siculus, 4.66; Hyginus, *Fabulae* 73; and Asclepiades, *FGrHist* 12 F 29 (= Schol. V. *Od*. 11.326), which I translate:

> Amphiaraus, son of Iocles, who married Eriphyle, daughter of Talaus, after quarrelling over some matters with Adrastus and then becoming reconciled, agreed with Adrastus to swear an oath that in any matters on which they might disagree they would entrust the decision to Eriphyle and obey her. Afterwards, when the expedition against Thebes took place, Amphiaraus tried to dissuade the Argives from it and prophesied the disaster which was to come, ⟨but Adrastus wanted the battle.⟩[2] Meanwhile Eriphyle, who had received the necklace of Harmonia from Polynices, declared to those who had been forced to assemble around Adrastus that Amphiaraus would join their expedition. When Amphiaraus found out about Eriphyle's receipt of the gift(s), he made violent accusation against her, and when he himself set out on the expedition, ordered Alcmaeon not to go to Thebes with

the Epigoni ("After-born") until he had killed his mother. It is said that Alcmaeon did all this and that he became mad because of the matricide, but that the gods released him from this sickness because in destroying his mother he was piously helping his father.

The following fragments are attributed to this play by ancient sources, or may be so attributed.

Attributed to Sophocles' *Epigoni*

Fr.188R. When men are attacked by envy, disgrace is wont to prevail, if their deeds are evil and not good.[3]
Fr.189R. O you wicked woman, wicked beyond measure, indeed there is and will be nothing worse than a woman, among the disasters which befall mortals.
Fr.190R. The man who will no longer live in the hollow of Argos.

Attributed to Sophocles' *Eriphyle*

Fr.201aR. O eloquence, you receive honour among men in whom words are stronger than deeds.
Fr.201bR. Where it is not permitted to say the best things freely, in that city wickedness prevails and mistakes ruin safety.
Fr.201cR. Keep a serene mind, as is seemly for old age.
Fr.201dR. The possession of virtue alone is a lasting thing.
Fr.201eR. For the courage of noble men does not grow soft.
Fr.201fR. How am I, who am mortal, to struggle against heaven-sent destiny? Where there is a danger, hope gives no help.
Fr.201gR. Depart! You disturb sleep, physician of disease.

Attributed to an *Epigoni* without Author's Name

Fr.185R. Accursed of children, what have you uttered?[4]
Fr.186R. Do you hear this, Amphiaraus, hidden under the earth?[5]
Fr.187R. Alc. You are akin to a husband-murdering wife.[6]
Ad. But you are slayer of the mother who bore you.

Attributed to Sophocles without Title

Fr.201hR. For I see the Argives (Eriphyle[2] to Alcmaeon).[7]

On the grounds stated in the following discussion I have also included the fragments of Accius' *Epigoni*[8] as available for the reconstruction of Sophocles' play, by accepting the views of Welcker, Ribbeck, Robert, and Mette.[9]

Frr.272–73W, How shall the eyes of any one of us / Be able to look those men in the face / Whom now at last their years keep back from warfare?
Fr.274W. Intelligence is ours through the mind; / Enjoyment, in our breath; when mind is absent / Breath is a thing enfeebled.
Fr.275W. And see you not the Argives roaring ''war''! / The rabble too all raving for riot?
Fr.276W. Thus bursts he out, a blunderer in stupidity, / A master of no counsel.
Frr.277–79W. But now I see Amphilochus coming towards us; / And so we are granted a welcome pause / In speaking, and time to return to camp.
Fr.280W. This too is the reason for my coming hither—/ That no man's ears should steal our words.
Fr.281W. Who grants no ending to my sad misfortunes / Unless I avenge my father.
Frr.282–83W. I do confess it; but why should I slacken / The advancement of this plan, or hesitate / To spare this person's life?

Frr.284–85W. Please tell me why, my only daughter, Demonassa, / You cry out and summon me frightened from the house?

Fr.286W. Speak out quickly and rid me of this fear of mine!

Fr.287W. I'll not / Delay to approach her. See! She is at hand. / How heavy with the neck-band is her throat!

Fr.288W. Don't you see how that disloyalty spurs you on, / And fear restrains you not!

Fr.289W. Don't! Don't! Get you away! Let go! / Best not touch the robe!

Fr.290W. Now will I proceed / To load the altars of the heavenly gods, / Appeasing them with worship.

Frr.291–93W. You will be near Glisas. Good luck in your banishment away from the lands of Pelops![10]

Fr.294W. Near by the plenteous-flowing age-old stream / And waters swift of Inachus.

There are two important questions to be discussed before a reconstruction can be attempted. First, is Accius Sophoclean? Second, is the *Eriphyle* of Sophocles to be identified with his *Epigoni,* as many critics have proposed?[11]

To begin with, let us look for some solid basis on which we may develop our discussion. We can extract two facts from the fragments of Accius' play: first, that there were two parties with opposed viewpoints concerning the expedition of the Epigoni, the agitators for war and the hesitant, who debated the issue on stage (Frr.275W, 272–73W, 277–79W, 276W); second, that a son appeared who felt oppressed by an obligation to his father (Fr.281W; note the word *miseriis*).

It would be natural for a son of Amphiaraus[12] to have felt great hesitation in supporting the prowar faction if he had been conscious of his father's command to kill his mother before the expedition could begin. Frr.277–79W, however, seem to show that Amphilochus, one of the two known sons of Amphiaraus, was wholeheartedly in favor of the war, since he is welcomed by those who have already shown us that they favor war. If Amphilochus was regarded as a reliable member of the prowar party, it could hardly have been he who was oppressed by a filial obligation. Who, then, could have spoken Fr.281W?

Tradition unanimously says that Alcmaeon slew his mother in obedience to his father's behest. But Apollodorus suggests that he was at first reluctant to do so. (See the quotation from Apollodorus.) In Diodorus (see below), Alcmaeon questions the oracle a second time, although the first oracle, obtained by other sons of the Seven (Epigoni), had already recommended the expedition and nominated Almaeon as the supreme commander. It is easily seen that Alcmaeon wanted to learn what the divine will would say about matricide. The second oracle, obviously to Alcmaeon's distress, sanctions both expedition and matricide. Mythographical descriptions can often be assumed to reflect the action of the tragedy, and we may conjecture that Alcmaeon was reluctant to support the expedition because he was afflicted with the idea of committing matricide beforehand, and that it was therefore Alcmaeon who spoke Fr.281W.[13] The injunction of matricide thus inseparably connected with the expedition, it would follow that the interlocutor or the opponent of the speaker of Frr.275W and 272–73W is Alcmaeon. The tragic design of the play then becomes very likely to be that the two brothers were opposed in their policy regarding the Theban expedition, Amphilochus actively promoting the idea of an attack and Alcmaeon holding back, and that Alcmaeon's reason for hesitation consisted of the emotional conflict between filial affection and the assigned duty of matricide.

Cicero (*Tusc*. 2.25.60) quotes a line from a Greek tragedy, *Epigoni* (Fr.186R): *Audisne haec, Amphiarae, sub terram abdite?*[14] There can be little doubt that the play he meant was Sophocles' *Epigoni* (see note 5). Cicero cites the line as spoken by Cleanthes, a disciple of Zeno who lived in the third century B.C., when Aeschylus' tragedies were out of fashion. Cleanthes shouted the words, striking the ground with his foot, at Dionysius of Heraclea, another disciple of Zeno, who had deviated from the doctrine of their deceased master by saying that pain was an evil. The meaning of the sentence is explained by an exact parallel to the supposed situation in Accius' *Epigoni:* that the sons of Amphiaraus are opposed to each other and one of them is infuriated by the words of the other, who has deviated from the will of their father, showing himself to be unwilling to execute paternal injunction. The injunction was the murder of Eriphyle, inseparably connected with the Theban expedition.[15] A scene of a violent break, as Fr.186R shows, would be highly probable, if such fraternal confrontation was part of the action.

Cicero writes elsewhere (*De opt. gen. orat.* 18): *Idem Andriam et Synephebos nec minus Terentium et Caecilium quam Menandrum legunt, nec Andromacham aut Antiopam aut Epigonos Latinos reiciunt: immo Ennium et Pacuvium et Accium potius quam Euripidem et Sophoclem legunt.* It is obvious that Cicero was wrong if he meant to say that Ennius' *Andromacha* is an adaptation of Euripides' extant play of the same title. Not only Cicero here but also Varro (*Ling.* 7.82) seems to take that view. But the fragments of Ennius' *Andromacha* show that the action falls soon after the capture of Troy.[16] On the other hand, he is probably right in regarding Pacuvius' *Antiopa* as a translation of the play of the same title by Euripides. That Pacuvius' *Antiopa* was modelled after Euripides' *Antiope* may be inferred from Hyginus (*Fab.* 8) and from Cicero (*Fin.* 1.2.4), who implies that the Roman poet followed the original fairly closely. Is Accius' *Epigoni* a translation of Sophocles? The discussion above leads us to suppose that Accius at least modeled his work on Sophocles in bringing about the confrontation of the brothers concerning the paternal injunction. Accius, as a whole, is said to have imitated his Greek models more faithfully than Pacuvius, and Pacuvius more than Ennius.[17] If the fraternal confrontation was borrowed from Sophocles, just as it was with Ismene and Antigone in

Antigona,[18] the consequent development of the action could not have been so very different from that in the original. If the reluctant hero is to succeed in performing his filial duty,[19] there cannot be many ways of reaching a dramatic solution. In all probability, therefore, Accius would have followed Sophocles in the development of the action.

The second question is whether the *Eriphyle* of Sophocles should be identified with his *Epigoni*. The most plausible argument for its identification with the *Epigoni* is that of Welcker, who argued that the tragic death of Eriphyle must be depicted in the tragedy that bears her name, while it is indisputable that the subject of Sophocles' *Epigoni* was her murder by Alcmaeon.

In Fr.281W it is explicitly stated that the paternal behest is also that of someone else. That divine will is meant may be inferred from mythographical descriptions. (Diodorus' second oracle mentioned below, Apollodorus as quoted below, and Asclepiades all testify to the divine will.) In Fr.201fR[20] of Sophocles, the speaker reveals his resigned acceptance of divine will, although he finds it unkind:[21] an interlocutor might be expected to be uttering his opposition to divine will. Immisch[22] was therefore certainly right to combine Accius' Fr.281W with Sophocles' Fr.201fR and state that the direction of the oracle was in accordance with the father's behest. But Ribbeck (491) was mistaken in thinking that Alcmaeon thus (Fr.201fR) surrendered himself to the divine will. While Fr.281W seems to preserve the words of Alcmaeon's protest, Fr.201fR, if my interpretation is right, must be spoken by Amphilochus to explain his own attitude toward the matricide. This is exactly the situation we now have guessed, through Accius, in Sophocles' *Epigoni*.

Fr.201fR comes from the *Eriphyle* of Sophocles. From a study of the mythographers, I can see that there is no other occasion when Fr.201fR could more suitably be spoken than as interpreted here. Fr.201fR fits exactly into the scene of an argument of the brothers with which the action of the *Epigoni* would have developed, inevitably to lead to an explosion as of Fr.186R. Fr.201fR may be thus taken to support Welcker's view.[23]

If persuasion by the Epigoni (Frr.272–73W, 275W) and the attack by Amphilochus (Frr.277–79W, 186R), supported by divine ordinance (Fr.201fR), did not break down the probable resolve of Alcmaeon, what could have swayed him into committing matricide, as he most probably did (Fr.187R)? I shall proceed by treating the *dramatis personae* in order to attempt to see how a dramatic solution could have been offered to the problem of the hero's probable refusal of filial duty, on the assumption that the fragments of Sophocles' *Eriphyle* and Accius' *Epigoni* are available for the elucidation of the probable dramaturgy of Sophocles' *Epigoni*.

Dramatis Personae

Eriphyle and Alcmaeon

Paroemiographi Graeci, App. Prov. 3.35 (Leutsch/ Schneidewin I 423) says: "Eriphyle was made by Sophocles to say to Alcmaeon καὶ γὰρ 'Αργείους ὁρῶ (Fr.201hR). It is said of those who are gazing at something iently and who are thought to be looking at something horrible." Although the title of the play is not stated, the exposition makes it very likely that it refers to Sophocles' *Epigoni*, indicating the critical moment when Alcmaeon was about to kill Eriphyle. Frr.284–85W show Eriphyle speaking. For further evidence for Alcmaeon's appearance, see below the discussion on Adrastus.

As to the time of Eriphyle's death, which certainly took place within the action of the play as Fr.187R shows, some critics have doubted that the matricide occurred before the expedition,[24] because Apollodorus writes (3.7.2ff): "Alcmaeon joined the expedition, though he was loath to lead the army till he had punished his mother; for Eriphyle persuaded her sons also to go to the war. . . . After the capture of Thebes, when Alcmaeon learned that his mother Eriphyle had been bribed to his undoing also, he was more incensed than ever and in accordance with an oracle given to him by Apollo he killed his mother. Some say that he killed her in conjunction with his brother Amphilochus, others that he did it alone.''[25]

The absurdity in Apollodorus is evident:[26] that Eriphyle should work such great power of persuasion over the sons who were determined to kill her or that Alcmaeon should postpone carrying out his father's command until he came back safe from the Theban expedition. The matricide then would no longer be a retribution for his wronged father but a tit-for-tat for his own self. Have we not seen that one point of the supposed tragic design lies in the conflicting emotions of Alcmaeon, to whom matricide before the expedition has been assigned as a filial duty? How could he have started out on the expedition, if one aspect of his tragedy consisted in his vascillation between filial affection and the enjoined duty of matricide, or at least compunction in refusing it, without having reached a decision about the problem? Eriphyle has to be murdered before the expedition. And if the discussion below on Adrastus is acceptable, Fr.187R assures us that the matricide was performed within the dramatic time.

Amphilochus

Frr.277–79W not only prove the appearance of Amphilochus, but also reveal his role in the play. The discussion above on Frr.281W, 201fR, and 186R suggests that his eagerness for battle was assumed not in ignorance of the assigned duty of matricide but in full awareness of its being the will of his father and the gods.

Thersander

There is no evidence to confirm his presence in the action. But the Epigoni were the bereaved sons of the Seven who attacked Thebes to help Polynices, who had been banished from his fatherland by his brother, Eteocles. Thersander is the son of Polynices. He is most naturally expected to be the most eager for the cause of the Theban expedition of the Epigoni and cannot be absent from the drama titled *Epigoni*.

Demonassa

It is unlikely that Demonassa, daughter of Eriphyle, addressed in Frr.284–85W, failed to appear onstage.[27] According to Pausanias (9.5.15), she is the wife of Thersander. There is no evidence, but it is quite probable that she was so represented in this play.[28] For if so, she would be the only person who could divulge the second bribery of Eriphyle, which is the only possible occasion for converting Alcmaeon from his refusal of matricide to its execution. Regrettably, there is no stronger suggestion in the play of the second bribery (Thersander presenting Eriphyle with the robe of Harmonia) having occurred than Fr.289W.[29] But if Alcmaeon showed such persistent reluctance that he caused the Epigoni to give up direct persuasion (Frr.277–79W) and provoked Amphilochus to argument (Fr.201fR) and rage (Fr.186R), could anything other than the disclosure of the second bribery cause him to commit matricide? Ribbeck (494) thought that the second bribery did not occur in the play, but, admitting that Alcmaeon at first showed signs of serious hesitation, he assumed (491) on the grounds of Fr.186R that the ghost of Amphiaraus appeared to direct Alcmaeon to matricide. Fr.186R, however, does not say anything about the appearance of the ghost.[30]

Welcker (272) accepts the second bribery as the direct cause that drives Alcmaeon to matricide. His view is grounded on Diodorus. But does Diodorus follow the actual sequence of the drama? In fact he writes: ". . . . But their sons, who were known as Epigoni, being intent upon avenging the death of their fathers, decided to make common cause in a campaign against Thebes, having received an oracle from Apollo that they should make war upon this city, and with Alcmaeon the son of Amphiaraus as their supreme commander. Alcmaeon, after they had chosen him to be their commander, inquired of the god concerning the campaign against Thebes and also concerning the punishment of his mother Eriphyle. And Apollo replied that he should perform both these deeds, not only because Eriphyle had accepted the golden necklace in return for bringing about the destruction of his father, but also because she had received a robe as a reward for securing the death of her son."[31] Diodorus does not proceed to tell whether Alcmaeon murdered Eriphyle in accordance with the oracle (he may have thought it evident from 4.65.7), but enters into a detailed description of the Epigoni's expedition. Was Welcker right in finding here a Sophoclean sequence and in assuming that the second bribery was revealed to Alcmaeon by the second oracle and that this drove Alcmaeon to matricide?

It is indeed very likely that the second oracle was consulted by Alcmaeon on the expedition and matricide during the play (Frr.280W? 286W?; but for other possibilities see note 46). What could it have told, and how could Alcmaeon have reacted? The oracle sanctioned the murder of Eriphyle, but it is very likely that Alcmaeon remained hesitant, whereas Amphilochus declared submission (Fr.201fR): "How am I, being mortal, to struggle against heaven-sent destiny, when hope gives no help in danger?" Alcmaeon as the interlocutor seems to be shown as refusing the paternal injunction, even now when he has learned that it is divine will. Fr.281W must also be uttered after the very probable inquiry of the second oracle. There, matricide is regarded only as the cruel will of the gods. If the second bribery had been disclosed by the second oracle, even Alcmaeon would have had to admit the justice of the divine injunction, but in fact he says that divine will is cruel: "Who grants no ending to my sad misfortune, unless I avenge my father."

We must conclude that the oracle, if it was consulted by Alcmaeon during the action of the play, did indeed sanction matricide but did not give any information about the second bribery. The information would have certainly been given in some other way, for there is no dramatic solution possible for the supposed procrastination of the matricide other than the information. The appearance of Demonassa, as wife of Thersander and sister of Alcmaeon, would be essential.

Adrastus

Plutarch cites (*De aud. poet.* 35E) a part of the dialogue in the *Epigoni* between Adrastus and Alcmaeon (Fr.187R). Antiphanes (Fr.191II 90K = Athen., 6.223) attests to Adrastus' appearance in the *Epigoni*. In neither case is the author's name given, but Sophocles' *Epigoni* is the only play likely to be referred to in these remarks. The contents of Aeschylus' *Epigoni* are not clear, but his play is much less likely to have been mentioned by a popular comic poet of the fourth century B.C.[32] There were other *Epigoni* plays,[33] but none of them is likely to have been referred to in this way. Moreover, it seems certain that the references of Plutarch and Antiphanes refer to the same feature of the play. Both speak of the emotional perturbation of Adrastus; presumably there was a famous scene between uncle and nephew after the matricide.[34]

Messenger

Eriphyle's murder may have been reported, as is the custom in Greek tragedy, by a messenger, unless Adrastus performed this role.

Chorus

The title suggests a chorus of the Epigoni.[35] Frr.277–79W consist of anapaests. In Sophocles' *Antigone,* there are remarkable anapaestic systems sung by the Chorus to introduce new characters or themes.[36] If Frr.277–79W are the words of the Chorus, they are of exactly the same type as these examples. The appearance of the Epigoni as the Chorus with some of their soldiers to fill the number would show that the Argives were demanding an expedition urgently.

The discussion of dramatis personae leads us to conjecture the probable course of action of the play: Alcmaeon was asked to become the commander of the Epigoni on their expedition against Thebes. He refused, because he had to murder Eriphyle before the expedition, in accordance with a paternal injunction. He consulted an oracle in the hope that it would not sanction matricide, but it did. Neither the demand of the Epigoni, nor the direction of heaven, nor the attack of Amphilochus turned him from his resolve. Disclosure of Eriphyle's second bribery was the only motive likely to lead to his breakdown. Demonassa was the only person who, as wife of Thersander, could discover it and who, as sister of Alcmaeon, felt constrained to disclose it. The disclosure converted the hero from obstinate refusal to a decision to commit matricide, and the murder took place. How could this probable course of action be handled in a tragedy of prologue, *epeisodia,* and *exodus* divided by choral odes? In presenting a tentative reconstruction of action I shall have to state as facts what is necessarily conjectural. The distribution of the roles would most appropriately be as the following:

Protagonist:	Alcmaeon	
Deuteragonist:	Eriphyle,	Amphilochus, and Adrastus
Tritagonist:	Demonassa,	Thersander, and Messenger

2

Tentative Reconstruction of the Action

Dramatic Time: Directly before the expedition[37] (Fr.275W and the discussion above on Eriphyle).

Dramatic Place: Argos, before the palace of Thersander (Frr.284–85). The palace of Thersander is more likely than that of Amphiaraus, for it would be difficult to engineer the presence of Demonassa at another palace.[38]

Prologue

There is no evidence to support any hypothesis on how the play opened, but it would be greatly detrimental, not only to the characterization of Alcmaeon but also to the progress of the action, to begin with the argument between the prowar party and Alcmaeon, who cannot disclose his real reason for avoiding the expedition. Sophocles must have composed the prologue in such a way that the predicament of Alcmaeon might be realized fully by the audience through his conversation with Amphilochus. A dialogue would be typical.[39] The audience must have been told about the treachery of Eriphyle, the subsequent death of Amphiaraus, his instructions of matricide and the Theban expedition, and Thersander's appeal to the authority of the oracle. Alcmaeon may have despatched Amphilochus to consult the oracle (the second oracle of Diodorus). It is Alcmaeon who goes to consult the oracle in Diodorus, where Amphilochus is never mentioned. In Sophocles' play, Amphilochus is the more likely of the two brothers to go to consult the oracle,[40] considering the probable sequence of events. *Trachiniae* provides a parallel to the prologue with dialogue exposition and the dismissal of one of the characters.[41]

33

First Episode

Thersander must come out himself together with the other Epigoni and attempt to persuade the reluctant Alcmaeon. Alcmaeon must have stubbornly refused to yield, arguing in general terms but not revealing the real reason for his hesitation. (If this did not happen, Thersander would not have had a sufficient motive for conceiving the bribery, which is assumable from Fr.289W, Diodorus, and Apollodorus, as cited above.) Three fragments of Accius seem to be spoken by Thersander.

> Frr.272–73W. . . . *Quibus oculis quisquam nostrum*
> *poterit illorum optui*
> *vultus, quos iam ab armis anni porcent?*
> Fr.275W. *Et nonne Argivos fremere bellum et velle*
> *vim vulgum vides?*
> Fr.274W. *Sapimus animo, fruimur anima; sine animo*
> *anima est debilis.*[42]

Alcmaeon cannot tell them the real reason for his refusal. Fr.201bR, Alcmaeon?[43]

> ὅπου δὲ μὴ τἄριστ᾽ ἐλευθέρως λέγειν
> ἔξεστι, νικᾷ δ᾽ ἐν πόλει τὰ χείρονα,
> ἁμαρτίαι σφάλλουσι τὴν σωτηρίαν

Fr.201aR, Thersander?

> ⟨ὦ⟩ γλῶσσ᾽, ἐν οἷσιν ἀνδράσιν τιμὴν ἔχεις,
> ὅπου λόγοι σθένουσι τῶν ἔργων πλέον

In Frr.277–79W, the arrival of Amphilochus is announced most probably by the Epigoni, who welcome his timely appearance and leave the persuasion up to him:[44]

34

Sed iam Amphilochum huc vadere cerno et
nobis datur bona pausa loquendi tempusque in
castra revorti.

If Amphilochus was welcomed on his first appearance before the Epigoni as a member of their side, he may have appeared in the prologue, as the deputy of Thersander and the Epigoni, to demand Alcmaeon's prompt acceptance of the command.

Frr.277–79W indicate the disappearance of the Epigoni, which enables the two brothers to hold a secret conversation on the answer of the oracle. Alcmaeon's brief reference to Thersander in his absence may be found in Fr.276W:[45]

Ita inperitus stupiditate erumpit se, impos consili.

But their conversation instantly turns to the oracle.
Fr.280W, Amphilochus?:

eaque ivi hoc causa ut nequis nostra verba
cleperet auribus.

Alcmaeon, Fr.286W?:[46]

Eloquere propere ac pavorem hunc meum expectora.

Alcmaeon must be shocked to learn that his father's command of matricide has been sanctioned by divine will.

Second Episode

In *Antigone,* assaults on Creon's resolve made by different characters are divided roughly into separate *epeisodia.* Analogy and the fragments (mainly Fr.186R) would allow us to conjecture

35

that the second episode was devoted to an *agon* of the brothers. Amphilochus, who seems to have been in favor of the expedition from the first, becomes all the more impetuous, if the matricide has been approved by divine will. He must have demanded that Alcmaeon accept the command without delay. Fr.281W may preserve the words of Alcmaeon expressing his dismay that Apollo has sanctioned matricide:[47]

qui nisi genitorem ullo, nullum meis dat finem miseriis.

Alcmaeon cannot bring himself to act. He may be hoping that with his help Eriphyle's degraded character would somehow be reformed. He may have conceived some plan of saving Eriphyle's life and revealed it to his brother (*haec* of Frr.282–83W). Amphilochus objects and confesses his acceptance of the matricide:[48]

Fr.201fR. πῶς οὖν μάχωμαι θνητὸς ὢν θείᾳ τύχῃ ;

ὅπου τὸ δεινόν, ἐλπὶς οὐδὲν ὠφελεῖ.

Amphilochus may call his brother defiant, finding him resisting the gods' authority, not only the paternal injunction. But Alcmaeon persists, Frr.282–83W (*huius* = Eriphyle):[49]

Fateor; sed cur proferre haec pigrem aut huius
dubitem parcere
capiti?

The *agon* perhaps concluded, as did the Haemon-Creon scene of *Antigone* (630–780), with Alcmaeon shaken but still determined not to give up. Fr.201eR would most appropriately be spoken by Alcmaeon defending his own beliefs.

ἀνδρῶν γὰρ ἐσθλῶν στέρνον οὐ μαλάσσεται

36

In Fr.186R, Amphilochus, enraged, calls to his dead father under the earth,

Audisne, haec, Amphiarae, sub terram abdite?

Amphilochus cannot remain inactive after the rupture. He may even have decided to kill Eriphyle himself if he is convinced that the gods will not grant them a successful expedition against Thebes unless Eriphyle dies.

Third Episode

Fr.201dR and a dubious fragment suggest that Alcmaeon earnestly admonishes Eriphyle: if Eriphyle saves herself from degradation, Aclmaeon's refusal to kill her may assume some validity. Alcmaeon must also be harassed by the fear that Amphilochus may anticipate him and attack his mother if he had exasperated Amphilochus at the end of the second episode (Fr.186R). His admonition, if it was in the play, is likely to take place after the appearance of Eriphyle, most fittingly at the beginning of the third episode.[50] Fr. 201dR must be a reference to the hollowness of possessing personal decoration, as Welcker (275) points out.[51]

ἀρετῆς βέβαιαι δ' εἰσὶν αἱ κτήσεις μόνης

Another fragment may also be from his admonition:[52] Fr.188R

φιλεῖ γὰρ ἡ δύσκλεια τοῖς φθονουμένοις
νικᾶν ἐπ' αἰσχροῖς ἢ 'πὶ τοῖς καλοῖς πλέον

Eriphyle's appearance could not have been an accident.[53] Her intention can only be to work Thersander's will upon

Alcmaeon. If direct persuasion had had to be dropped because of its lack of effect (Frr.277–79W) in what I call for the sake of reconstruction the first episode, Thersander may have bribed Eriphyle during the second episode, and Eriphyle could have presented herself before Alcmaeon if she had known him to be an affectionate son and been convinced that she could prevail upon him to accept the expedition's leadership. (The implication of Eriphyle's appearance before Alcmaeon would instantly be realized by the spectators if she wore the fabulous robe (Fr.289W) as well as the necklace (Fr.287W). Sophocles, who displayed so much skill in using stage properties, could hardly have neglected an opportunity to bring the robe, if she had accepted it from Thersander, onto the stage in his favorite ironic situation:[54] Eriphyle, decorated with the dazzling ominous ornaments, appears with the hidden intention of sending her own son to perilous battle, and the son, quite ignorant of the new treachery, desperately tries to admonish her.)

Amphilochus cannot afford to be slow in pursuing his plot if he broke off with his brother at the end of the second episode. He must have been searching for Eriphyle, with his murderous intention obvious to all. The imminent danger is announced by the shout of Demonassa, who could appear with appropriate reason if the dramatic place was before the palace of Thersander. For what else could have been meant by her shout implied in Frr.284–85W, spoken by Eriphyle:

> *Quid istuc, gnata unica, est, Demonassa, obsecro,*
> *quod me . . . expetens timidam e tecto excies"?*

Eriphyle may quickly exit. In any case, the appearance of Demonassa must lead to the disclosure to Alcmaeon of Eriphyle's second bribery. (He must at first be reluctant to believe Demonassa's words, but if he has already seen the robe on Eriphyle, all denial is precluded.) At last, Alcmaeon, now converted, professes his decision to kill Eriphyle, Fr.189R:[55]

ὦ πᾶν σὺ τολμήσασα καὶ πέρα, γύναι.

κάκιον ἀλλ' οὐκ ἔστιν οὐδ' ἔσται ποτὲ

γυναικός, εἴ τι πῆμα γίγνεται βροτοῖς

Fourth Episode

Eriphyle is now aware that unless she sends her sons off promptly on the expedition, the threat to her own life is imminent. She must appear again, to influence or even to entreat Alcmaeon and, dramatically, to be murdered by him. But Alcmaeon is now determined to kill his mother.[56] Fr.287W, Alcmaeon unseen by Eriphyle?

> . . . Quid cesso ire ad eam? Em praesto est; camo collum gravem![57]
> (Fr.326W. Pallas bicorpor anguium spiras trahit.)[58]

Eriphyle notices Alcmaeon's murderous intention and switches to defence: she must remind Alcmaeon of filial feeling, Fr.288W,[59]

> Viden ut te inpietas stimulat nec moderat metus?

Fr.185R:

ὀλόμενε παίδων, ποῖον εἴρηκας λόγον; [60]

Alcmaeon is about to catch and kill her. Eriphyle's words Fr.289W:

> Age age amolire! Amitte! Cave vestem attigas![61]

It is recorded that Eriphyle, when driven into the corner, suddenly gazed at a point in the air and shouted Fr.201hR:

καὶ γὰρ Ἀργείους ὁρῶ

The sentence was later applied to those who seemed to have a hallucination.[62] If Eriphyle is being terrified by an illusory sight of the Argives, they cannot be perceived as hurrying to save her from Alcmaeon's murderous sword, as Ribbeck thought, refuted by Pearson.[63] The Argives must rather be coming to join Alcmaeon in his attack. If the horror-stricken words of Eriphyle make Alcmaeon flinch for a moment, Eriphyle can rush off and Alcmaeon may run after her. The murder must take place offstage.

Exodus

If Adrastus really appeared in Sophocles' *Epigoni*,[64] a short but violent dispute with Alcmaeon must have occurred after the announcement by the messenger of Eriphyle's death, Fr.187R:

> ALC. ἀνδροκτόνου γυναικὸς ὁμογενὴς ἔφυς.
>
> ADR. σὺ δ' αὐτόχειρ γε μητρὸς ἥ σ' ἐγείνατο.

Not only is the great indignation of Adrastus remarkably recorded here (see above on Adrastus), but Alcmaeon, too, must have been a passionate speaker throughout the play. Cicero (*Off.* 1.31, 114) says that the role was taken up eagerly by an actor with a loud voice. This may be a fragment from the harsh exchange of words between uncle and nephew, Fr.201cR:

> γήρᾳ προσῆκον σῷζε τὴν εὐφημίαν [65]

Immisch[66] supposed, and it is very probable, that the famous melody that had the reconciliatory effect mentioned by Philodemus (*De musica* 1. 30 Kemk.) was sung after the dispute between uncle and newphew. Adrastus left the stage quickly (Athen., 6.223).

Fr.290W seems to be best placed here as words of Alcmaeon, eager to allay the gods' rage:

Nunc pergam ut suppliciis placans caelitum aras
expleam.[67]

Alcmaeon's insanity after the matricide is recorded unanimously by tradition. Madness can be represented in Greek tragedy as a short fit to be cured by sleep,[68] and Fr.201gR suggests such a sequence:

ἄπελθε· κινεῖς ὕπνον ἰατρὸν νόσου [69]

The speaker could be Amphilochus trying to disperse this fit of madness.

Robert (959) concluded from Asclepiades that Alcmaeon did not require purification by the hand of a human, because his deed had been filial and sanctioned by Apollo. If the gods soon released Alcmaeon from insanity, as Asclepiades records, he would have commanded the army successfully. This settles the doubt of Pearson and others as to how a mad general could have led the army on an expedition to Thebes.[70] This way of treating Alcmaeon's insanity is dramatically preferable to the traditional purification by Phegeus in Psophis.

Robert supposed Apollo *ex machina* to declare the release from madness and the future victory of the expedition, on the grounds of Athenaeus, 6.222b, but that passage does not seem to relate to this particular play. If Amphilochus, however, was shown to inherit Amphiaraus' art of prophecy,[71] he could more suitably foretell these things. In Frr.291–93W, Bergk's brilliant conjecture has restored the name of Glisas, the scene of the decisive battle fought between the Epigoni and the Thebans:[72]

Maneas ad Glisantem, exilio macte ex terris
Pelopiis!

41

Fr.294W and Fr.190R may also come from this scene, but this cannot be decided with certainty.

Fr.294W. *apud abundantem antiquam amnem et rapidas undas Inachi.*
Fr.190R.

τὸ κοῖλον ᾿Αργος οὐ κατοικήσουτ᾿ ἔτι [73]

3

Epigoni is a tempting but difficult play to reconstruct, with everything further obscured through Accius and the two titles. The main problem throughout is the lack of testimonia for the action. The reconstruction here attempted is only a hypothesis based on assumption, often of unprovable relevance. But if the general contour of the drama as outlined here is acceptable as being consistent with the evidence available, it would be reasonable to think about the possibility of an aspect of Sophoclean tragedy that is too often neglected or even forgotten: a change of heart of a hero.

The story itself offers a suitable medium by means of which the moral quandary of a matricide could be dramatically represented. Sophocles wrote a play on another famous matricide story, and it is fully preserved: *Electra*. But in that tragedy, the heroine appears as obsessed almost morbidly with the idea of vengeance upon her mother, tied hand and foot to what she believes to be filial obligation to her father. She is quite happy to fulfil her purpose in the face of series of adversary factors. Nor does Orestes, her brother, waver onstage between acceptance and refusal of what Apollo prophesied and what justice demands, as he asserts. In fact, few other tragic characters have elicited more criticism than the Orestes of Sophocles' *Electra*, who betrays not a bit of doubt about the enjoined work of matricide and who accomplishes it with such efficiency and eagerness. No other ending of a play has been more embarrassing than the triumphant, happy ending of a murderous story where a dreadful deed is done as if it were something praiseworthy.

Alcmaeon has sufficient—indeed, more than sufficient—external incentive to commit matricide, as the gist of the legendary story tells us. However, if *Epigoni* was not very different from the play as outlined here, the hero most probably refuses his obligation of matricide at first (Fr.186R, Frr.277–79W, assuming that the Theban expedition is inseparably connected with the matricide, *cf.* Apollod: "though he was loath to lead the army till he had punished his mother") but changes his mind and kills his mother (Fr.187R). It is possible that what the poet puts aside in *Electra,* he comes to grips with in *Epigoni.* We may therefore state, tentatively, that the subject of the *Epigoni* is the suffering and resistance and a final change of heart of a hero who has been commanded to kill his own mother by paternal will (and divine direction).

It may be right to say that Sophocles has not shown in his extant plays a heroic soul at bewildering cross-purposes with itself. (Philoctetes' hesitation in *Philoctetes* (1350, 1352) makes a significant exception.) The hallmark of a Sophoclean hero is seen in the stubborn way he sticks to his guns, no matter what force is rallied against him. Ajax, Antigone, and other "Sophoclean" heroes all show a defiant and persistent resistance against overbearing authorities and earnest supplication.

Schadewaldt saw in Medea's monologue in Euripides' *Medea* a protagonist of Greek drama for the first time talking to herself in a thorough discussion of the question, resisting her own passion, which thwarts her former design, revealing all the emotional conflicts, and reaching a conclusion through her own judgments.[74] Knox observes that this constant shift of mind is the new trend of Euripides and his age, which could not afford to accept the one fixed attitude of heroic fortitude promoted by Aeschylus and Sophocles.[75]

We cannot tell whether Alcmaeon revealed any of the conflicting passions in his soul by hesitation, indecision, procrastination, or reluctance. Yet we may well imagine Alcmaeon's soul torn and tattered. For it is a tragic dilemma in the truest sense of the word that a son has to kill his mother by the command of his father. It is conjecturable that the divine injunction was emphatically used by the playwright to enhance the dramatic effect of the suffering of the hero (Fr.201fR, Fr.281W, Apollod., Diod.). The skillful use of oracles in Sophocles' drama to bring into high relief the fear and anxiety of the characters involved in tragic situation is always the marvel of critics. The public cause of Theban expedition would have added, dramatically, to the agony of making a difficult moral decision or sticking to it. Arguments and assaults would have been made to try to shake him (Fr.272-73W, Fr.275W, Fr.201aR, Apollod., Diod.). In any case, he kills his mother (Fr.187R). We may therefore advance our discussion on the assumption that, even though a Sophoclean hero, Alcmaeon *does* change his mind.

It is argued that Creon in *Antigone,* who shows as much heroic firmness and devotion to one idea as any other Sophoclean hero, is the protagonist of the play.[76] His antagonism against Antigone based on the principle of the stately order of a *polis,* his belief and self-destruction in defence of it, is no less heroic than that of other heroes of Greek drama. He is onstage longer than Antigone.

On the other hand, the champions of Antigone recognize in her that typically Sophoclean heroic quality and see a lack of heroic stature and tragic dignity in Creon. They detect a weakness in his change of mind. When Teiresias says that Creon has angered the gods and that the Erinyes will strike (1064–1076), he is staggered (1095). He asks the Chorus what to do (1099). The

Chorus advise him to yield (1103). Creon accepts (1105–1106). He repeals his pride and obduracy with two lines of compunction. Knox has noticed that his change of mind is voiced in passive forms of expression or in words with passive connotations.[77] It may be asserted that this passivity above all other characteristics makes him a secondary character beside Antigone's heroic courage, despite the latter's condemned and lonely situation.

Whether the one view is more influential or the other less enthusiastically supported, the serious debate that attempts to defend either side bears clear witness to the importance of the matter.[78] Whether Creon's part was played by a protagonist or not, the existence of a major character in an extant play who has made a decision but changes his mind after long perseverance should not be overlooked.

If some more lost plays of Sophocles have been as lucky as the surviving seven, we may place Creon, and Alcmaeon, in a clearer position. Professor Calder reconstructed *Polyxene* and found that Agamemnon appeared as a king who, out of compassion, could not consent to sacrificing a Trojan princess (Polyxene) to Achilles, but who finally gave his permission.[79]

According to Calder, Achilles' ghost first emerges to reveal his indignation, saying that his prominent contribution to the Greek cause has not been properly rewarded and demanding the sacrifice of Polyxene (Fr.523R). His wrath prevents the sailing of the Greek ships. Only the sacrifice can stop it. Menelaus enters to confront his brother (Strabo, 10.3.14), whose philanthropism restrains him from allowing this cruel human sacrifice. Odysseus (or Neoptolemus) next appears to make his request, only to leave the king shaken in his resolve but not converted. Agamemnon compares his plight to that of Zeus, who as a ruler cannot be generous to everyone (Fr.524R).[80] The play (dated by Calder *ca.* 450 B.C.) is interpreted by Calder as a prototype tragedy of the ruler who, after a long qualm, changes his mind, achieving much greater success about ten years later in *Antigone*.

As in *Antigone,* where Creon remains determined to have his way in spite of the attacks first by Antigone, then by Ismene and Haemon, he ultimately gives up struggling against the inevitable when Teiresias reveals the imminent loss of a kindred person in exchange for the body Creon has cast underground alive (1068), so in the same way in *Polyxene* Agamemnon finally changes his mind at the admonition of Calchas, who conveys the will of heaven. Polyxene is sacrificed, and the Greek army with Agamemnon are about to depart when Achilles' ghost reemerges, grateful, to foretell the dreadful incident awaiting the king at home (Frr.525R and 526R).

If the tragic pattern that Calder saw in *Antigone,* deriving from *Polyxene,* could also be suspected in *Epigoni* with a hero changing his mind after a persistent refusal under mental pressure, such a hidden stream of an essentially tragic theme in Sophoclean drama cannot be ignored. *Epigoni,* if it had had Alcmaeon as a hero forced to make a decision between two difficult choices and eventually making a drastic conversion from one decision to another, would have shown a different side of Sophocles, who, though usually understood as a begetter of rigid and monolithic souls, has included in his idea of a tragic hero something humane, responsive, and vulnerable.

At the same time, one should not be surprised if Alcmaeon's madness, which can be safely inferred from Fr.201gR (*cf.* Asclepiades: he became mad because of the matricide) as preceding a sleep scene, was so depicted that the audience felt it to be a necessary consequence of the immense suffering of a hero who went through an immeasurably tormenting ordeal, not simply as a mechanical sequence following abnormal events.

So far as we know from Greek literary tradition, madness in Greek thinking is something imposed on a man from an external source;[81] a manic fit is a divine visitation. The derangement of Ajax (*Ajax* 185, 278–80) and Heracles (in *Heracles Furens* 822–73 and 922ff) is induced after the introduction of particular deities who send it to them.[82] As in *Choephoroi* (1050ff) and *Eumenides* (the opening scene) Orestes is harassed by the pursuit of the Erinyes, so in this play the goddesses of revenge are expected to be represented and to begin to work promptly in one form or another. Nevertheless, Alcmaeon's insanity would not have seemed a mere daemonical possession that conventional patterns of thinking can explain away.

One may think that Alcmaeon has every reason in the world to undertake the murder of Eriphyle (see note 13, of chapter 5). There is no defending a woman who drove her husband to destruction in exchange for a pretty necklace. A son's filial duty to his mother would not be regarded as more important than that to his father in a tradition in which paternal principles definitely dominate.[83] In more general terms, there are at least three valid reasons for sanctioning this matricide: first, the dead man's wish to be revenged; secondly, *Dike* which does not allow the perturbed order of the world to be left unrectified; third, the call of the Erinyes (the goddesses of revenge) of "blood for blood," which functions somewhat more mechanically and automatically than *Dike,* standing for the more primitive and darker aspects of the forces in the world.[84]

However, it seems very likely that Alcmaeon could not bring himself to engage in matricide, as Fr.186R as interpreted above with other relevant documents would suggest. If he chose to stand against divine will, the one single source of his persistence would have been his affection to the mother who bore and nourished him. The supposed first decision of Alcmaeon could therefore torment him a great deal.

Once he has killed his mother, he will not be exempted from the charge of matricide, even though paternal will demanded the action. Alcmaeon is called "a slayer of the mother who bore you" (Fr.187R). Matricide, without doubt, is culpable from the human moral viewpoint. Even if the oracle had been in agreement, divine order would not have shielded him from pollution.

We do not know how the anguish of a man who, probably after a serious emotional vacillation, has negated one of the most fundamental of human relationships could have been dramatically expressed, except that Alcmaeon became mad (Fr.201gR). Although the original play is lost and much of what I have said is inevitably based on speculation, we may at least say with some degree of probability that Sophocles could have introduced a sensitive heart quite different from Orestes and Electra in his other play about matricide, without omitting the insanity but enclosing it as an integral and meaningful part of his version.

Can we find any hints for the discussion of chronology? In *Electra* 845 Amphiaraus is mentioned as a spirit demanding retribution from below the earth. One may well suppose that the passage could be a reference to his own *Epigoni,* but this inevitably remains a mere guess.

If Accius' anapaests in Frr.277–79W reflect Sophoclean ones, their similarity to passages from *Antigone* would suggest an early composition.[85] It is indeed very dangerous to discuss chronology on the basis of Roman testimonia. It may be suspected that the Roman poet was much more independent of the Greek model in his treatment of the Chorus than he was in his treatment of the actors' parts.[86]

The theme of fraternal confrontation on the problem of family duty, which, in the form of a strong sister in opposition to a weak sister, constitutes one important factor of the dramatic success of *Antigone,* was utilized in *Electra.* Certainly the device was one of the favourite techniques of Sophocles throughout his dramatic career.

Archaeological evidence does not help. We must regrettably admit that no definite clue to dating can be found.

If, nevertheless, the contents of the play as here suggested approximate to any extent to what Sophocles actually wrote, we may not be led amiss to think that the poet's notion of tragic heroism did not rule out those mental qualities that are not altogether similar to those of his existing heroes. If *invincibility, spiritual triumph,* and *self-realization* were the words that represent them, was the man who changed his mind, killed his mother, and went mad regarded by the dramatist as inadequate to dominate the stage of his tragedy? Did the poet find a change of heart unsuitable to his hero? That he did not seems to be the fact, if the course of the action I postulated had something indicative of the dramatic construction of the play.

Epigoni was one of Sophocles' most famous plays and well-accepted by immediate posterity (*cf.* note 5) but was not ''selected'' to be one of the surviving plays. We must then remember how much of Sophocles we have lost and be cautious in our understanding of his idea of tragic heroism by not putting too much emphasis on the apparent homogeneity of his extant drama. The lost Sophocles may have contained much which the ''selector'' did not find typically ''Sophoclean,'' but was fully appreciated by the poet's contemporary audience and succeeding ages.

If my attempt to restore, tentatively, a play that has come down to us only in an extremely small number of fragments has been in some degree helpful in letting us give thought to a neglected side of the poet in our quest for the essence of his dramatic poetry, we may proceed to examine another lost play. But the poor quality and quantity of the majority of Sophocles' fragments do not allow us to extend our discussion directly into an adjacent area. The play for the next chapter is chosen mainly because we have more information here than about most of the other lost plays of Sophocle: *Tereus,* a story of a daughter of an Athenian king, married to a Thracian, who killed her own son out of folly (*Od.* 19.523) and was metamorphosed into a nightingale.

If a careful examination of the fragments would enable us to see some more aspects of Sophocles, long lost and forgotten but reclaimable and ascertainable, we may further proceed and ask a question: how is the poet likely to have explored the legend as a paradigm of man's condition? How is it related to the problem of Sophocles' tragic heroism?

It can easily happen that we assume the creator of the heroes, all uniformly characterized as rigid and strict, to be likewise rigid and strict. We shall see if he was so in chapter 3, where the question will be propounded from the viewpoint of Sophocles' attitude toward the non-Greek world, because the material and its probable dramatic handling demand us to pursue our inquiry, first, along that line.

3

Sophocles and the
Non-Greek World: *Tereus*[1]

1

Of the three great tragedians, Sophocles is thought to be the one least interested in barbarians.[2] Two facts may be responsible for this wrong assumption.

First, he did not introduce in his extant plays as many barbarian characters and objects as did Aeschylus and Euripides. But it is rash to say that he was a classical, purely Greek poet with no concern at all about other races, when only seven plays are left to us out of a total of one hundred and twenty-three that Sophocles wrote.[3] The seven plays were selected by someone unknown in the second century A.D., so supposed Wilamowitz in 1875,[4] for use in schools, and through the same procedure seven were chosen from Aechylus and ten from Euripdes. (The survival of the other nine plays of Euripides must have been a fluke. They happened to be kept in roughly alphabetical order in one medieval manuscript.) Some modification has been made on this proposition:[5] that the "selection" was, so to speak, an approval of what the reading public up to that time had favored, rather than an entirely new evaluation. Of Euripides, it has been suggested that the availability of commentaries must have been an important factor in the plays' having acquired popularity, in addition to the taste of the reading public, and that the codex form that accommodated seven to ten plays each may have helped the popular "selection" to outlive the rest. The idea that popularity more or less played a part in the selection may urge one to regard the surviving plays as epitomizing the whole drama of the poet, but popular taste, when kept in check by educational intention, may repudiate what is unpleasant and unwelcome to civilized human society. Anyway, the proportion of the surviving plays to the entire number of works is the smallest in Sophocles' case.[6] We should be justified in hesitating over a decision that the seven extant plays represent the sum total of Sophoclean tragedy.

Secondly, the traditional idea of Sophocles as a symbol of the Athenian cultural florescence, arising partly from anecdotal pieces of information about his life, has led us to believe that he was not interested in the world outside Athens.[7] It is what one would expect of a man whose span of life exactly covers the golden age of Athenian prosperity. He was born some five years before the miraculous victory at Marathon (497 or 496 B.C. Marm. Par.). He grew up with the rise of the fortune of Athens. He died as an old man (406 or 405 B.C., Marm. Par.) one year before the Athenian citizens saw the Piraean Wall demolished by the Spartan soldiers. Compared to contemporary men of distinction who, more or less, suffered a cold reception from their fellow citizens, with vulgar accusation, misunderstanding, and the tensions caused by rivalry and so on,[8] Sophocles had an exceptionally happy life, experiencing both fame and success, loved and respected by everybody.[9] He is reported never to have left his beloved home country except once when he went to Samos in the capacity of a general, together with Pericles.[10] Sophocles performed important state offices.[11] With his popularity and ability to produce one play about every six months on the average, he may have had neither the time nor the need to travel abroad. One would not be surprised if such a man remained indifferent to different races and things in remote parts of the world.

However, if we look at the fragments of Sophocles, it will be clear that he was not only deeply interested in foreign peoples but actually introduced many of them and their ways of life in his lost plays. Sophocles dramatized the story of Andromeda and visualized the Ethiopian world, albeit with topographical errors, and was perhaps the first poet of Greek tragedy to do so.[12] References to a number of exotic musical instruments are to be found in the fragments of *Thamyras* (Frr.238R, 241R), in which the principal character was a renowned Thracian lyrist. We know that Medea, a Colchian princess, played a large part in at least three lost plays of Sophocles: *Colchides* (attested in Schol. Ap. Rhod. 3.1040), *Rhizotomoi* (Macrobius, *Sat.* 5.19.8 = 534R) and *Scythai* (*cf.* Schol. Ap. Rhod. 4.223 = 546R). Plays with the Trojans as leading or important characters are numerous: *Laocoon, Alexander, Antenoridae, Troilus,* and so on. When he describes Triptolemus' itinerary in *Triptolemus* (Frr.598R, 600R, 601R, 602R, 604R), the brilliance of his language provides for the audience an absolutely satisfying feeling of reality. His references to Egyptian domestic life in *Oedipus Coloneus* (337–41) and Scythian barbarian customs in *Oinomaos* (Fr.473R) betray his own interest and stimulate the audience's curiosity about life in alien places. It is evident that he was genuinely interested in the non-Greek world and tried to be as specific and accurate as possible in dealing with different peoples and their way of life.

Sophocles' knowledge of barbarians is largely attributed to Herodotus. There is no direct testimony that proves that they were personal acquaintances, but Herodotus seems to have been in Athens around the middle of the 440s.[13] It is recorded that Herodotus read his books before an audience in an Athenian gathering (Euseb., *Chron.* s.01.83,4 = 445/4 B.C. = I.113. 16-17 Helm). Prominent figures of the city, including Sophocles, must have been there, and it is also very likely that Herodotus may have shown the poet some parts of his manuscripts or talked personally to him about things outside the Greek world. The widely travelled Ionian would have been, to the thoroughbred Athenian poet, not only a valuable supplier of information about the unknown world but also a subject of keen interest and profound admiration. Sophocles composed a poem in praise of Herodotus.[14] The close spiritual kinship has been thoroughly studied.[15]

One notable characteristic of Herodotus that must have impressed Sophocles would have been his liberalism. His observation of the vast human world had endowed Herodotus with remarkable open-mindedness.[16] His Ionian origin may also have helped to suggest a conception of the world different from that of the mainland Greek.[17] In his *Historiae* (7.102), he proudly proclaims that wisdom and respect for the law (or usage of custom) have distinguished the Greeks from other peoples, and yet his reports on various races, unfamiliar customs, strange gods and their worship, unknown natural phenomena, and so on are delivered with such enthusiasm and vigor that the reader is immediately infected with his encyclopedic curiosity and passion. The reader understands his high regard of the immemorial oriental tradition. Herodotus was a patriot and, at the same time, was rightly called pro-barbarian.[18]

It is difficult to decide just when the opposition between Greeks and non-Greeks began to loom up in Greek consciousness. Thucydides infers (1.3) from the fact that the word *barbaroi* does not appear in the *Iliad* except once, as a compound *barbarophonoi* (speaking foreign tongues, 2.867) that there was no collective term for all the Greeks or one for the non-Greeks as its opposite. Strabo objects (14.2. 28), arguing on the grounds of the same reference, and the two interpretations are still reasserted by modern critics.[19] But it is at least certain that Homer did not expressly state a notion of Greek contempt toward barbarians.[20] Nobody would disagree that it was the Persian War that gave a speedy and definite rise to the general sentiment of Greek superiority.

The unprecedented crisis brought about by the huge oriental

empire excited the racial consciousness of the Greeks as a whole. The narrow victory over their powerful enemy awakened them to their capacity and position. Aeschylus, as the warrior of the glorious Marathon battle, could not but applaud Greek values. Seeking to establish new ideals for a new *polis*-state, he showed what was desirable in man and society. He condemned moral failure and injustice. In his *Persae,* the Athenians' independence and fortitude (241ff, 400ff) are pushed to the fore against emotional indulgence, lack of political freedom, tyrannical despotism, and the unbalanced luxury of the Persian monarchy. But, remarkably enough in view of the temptation to ''jingoism'' offered by the theme and proximity of the historical events, the Persians, apart from the infatuated Xerxes, are treated with surprising dignity. In *Supplices,* modesty, self-control, self-reliance, and frankness, personified in Pelasgus, are admired as Greek values.[21] But the dismay and the sad plight of the Danaids are depicted with a touch of heart-felt sympathy. When Aeschylus uses the word *barbaroi* (*e.g., Sept.,* 463, *Ag.* 919), we feel that foreign subjugation is disapproved of in contrast to free, enterprising Greek spirit. Nevertheless, we must admit that barbarian inferiority is not necessarily indicated. The barbarians, in their speech and behavior, are so vividly and vigorously portrayed, so carefully and realistically drawn, that they give us the impression that the poet takes great delight in depicting their life. We must say that Aeschylus presented the foreign world as something fascinating, worthy of serious concern.[22]

Euripides, Herodotus' contemporary, was no exception to the Greek tragedians who could not write without taking into account the theme of the Greek-barbarian relationship, since they used Greek myth as the basis of their work. His contact with Herodotus is more than probable. It is hard to imagine that the famous Athenian poet did not meet the historian in Athens. But no record tells us about anything akin to friendship between Euripides and Herodotus. It is suggested that some Euripidean words and remarks are derived from Herodotus.[23] He may have taken plots and ideas from Herodotus, yet his mentality seems to be quite different from that of Herodotus. Euripides' concern is in the domain of ideas rather than of facts, and his sentiments tend to be expressed as abstractions and symbols. Euripides discusses, sometimes eagerly, the relative merits of Greek and barbarian culture. There are, indeed, a large number of foreign geographical references. Many barbarian characters appear in his drama. But where we might expect a local touch, his approach turns out to be thematic and general. Thoas in *Iphigenia in Tauris* and Theoclymenos in *Helena* are not actually Taurian and Egyptian, but symbolic barbarian kings used expediently to produce an effect of outlandishness, exoticism, and unreality. Frequent references to the temple of Tauric Artemis are not very much different from the expression applied to the temple of Apollo at Delphi in *Ion*. The Egyptian palace and tomb in *Helena* (70, 430, 1165), Polymestor's Thracian attire in *Hecuba* (1153–1154), Dionysus' tour in *Bacchae* (13–20), and Hermione's deprecation of Asian custom in *Andromache* (170ff) give us very little information about actual foreign life, manners, places, and institutions. As Bacon summarised,[24] "the great store of information about Phrygia, Colchis, Tauris, Egypt, Ethiopia was left almost untouched."

It has been observed that Sophocles is more realistic and individual than Euripides in his portrayal of foreigners.[25] If we find any sign of Sophocles' trying to represent the barbarians not as a generalized mass of foreign people, but carefully distinguishing local qualities and differentiating between peoples with different racial propensities, we must modify our view of Sophocles as a "purely Greek poet" not concerned with the foreign world. On examination of a lost play with a barbarian in his title role, *Tereus,* Sophocles will be found, as it seems, to be akin to Herodotus, who was second to none in his love for his country and yet was free from racial prejudice. He took such pride in the Greek observance of law, but at the same time could fully ap-

56

preciate oriental experiences. We may perhaps assume that Herodotean liberalism must have been assimilated with Sophoclean literature in one form or another.

2

Sophocles, in taking up the story of Tereus, seems to have been particularly conscious of the Greek-barbarian antithesis.[26] The legend of the two Athenian sisters who were metamorphosed into a nightingale and a swallow on account of their abominable conduct towards Tereus had been popular enough to be mentioned casually by the poets before and during the fifth century B.C.[27] Since Aelian (*Var. hist.* 12.20) suggests that Hesiod referred to the vigil of the nightingale as the consequence of the impious banquet (Fr.125Rz), the legend must have included both the husband's crime and the wife's vengeance when Sophocles found dramatic material in it. No other great tragedian except Sophocles seems to have dramatized it. For Aristophanes, in *Aves* 281, made the Chorus say to a hoopoe (crested bird), referring to another, which had newly appeared, "Then you were not the only hoopoe but here is another!" The first hoopoe replies, "He is one produced from Philocles' hoopoe. I am his grandfather." The scholiast comments on this passage: "Sophocles first produced *Tereus* and then Philocles. Accordingly he said, 'I am his grandfather' instead of 'I wrote before him.' " Aristophanes joked that Philocles, writing a tetralogy titled *Pandionis* on the Tereus story, plagiarized Sophocles. We may safely assume that Sophocles' *Tereus* created a topic and gave a decisive form to the legend.[28]

Parsons published in 1974 a papyrus hypothesis of "Tereus" which he thought could be a hypothesis (synopsis) to Sophocles' play.[29] The existence of a collection of hypotheses was suggested by Wilamowitz in 1875, though only for Euripides.[30] The proposition was proved when in 1933 Gallavotti published papyrus fragments of Euripidean hypotheses (*Rhesus, Rhadamanthys,* and

Scyrioi).[31] It was further corroborated by succeeding publications,[32] and more are yet to come. The Tereus hypothesis is one that cannot be attributed to Euripides, as he most certainly did not write on this subject. Although the text has clear marks of having come through a long history of abridgment and tailoring to meet the requirements of editors who used it, its similarity, still recognizable, to the Euripidean hypotheses[33] suggests that the hypothesis descends from the same author. Haslam assumed this was the author Dicaearchus, a pupil of Aristotle and contemporary of Theophrastus.[34] Dicaearchus wrote *Hypotheses of the Dramatic Plots of Euripides and Sophocles*. The book seems to have remained standard down to the end of the second century A.D.[35] Meanwhile, there is very little difference among the descriptions of Tereus' story by mythographers,[36] which suggests that they derive from one common source. It would be most reasonable to accept Haslam and regard the Tereus hypothesis as one descending from Dicaearchus, who wrote on going back to Sophocles' original play. Parsons renders:

> Pandion, the ruler of the Athenians, having daughters, Procne and Philomela, united the elder, Procne, in marriage with Tereus the King of the Thracians, who had by her a son whom he named Itys. As time passed, and Procne wished to see her sister, she asked Tereus to travel to Athens to bring [her back]. He, after reaching Athens and receiving the girl from Pandion and making half the return journey, fell in love with the girl. And he disregarded his trust and violated her. But, as a precaution in case she should tell her sister, he cut out the girl's tongue. On arriving in Thrace, and Philomela being unable to speak her misfortune, she revealed it by means of a piece of weaving. When Procne realized the truth, driven mad by jealousy . . . she took Itys and killed him and after cooking him served him up to Tereus. He ate the meal without realizing. The women took flight and became, one of them a nightingale, one a swallow, and Tereus a hoopoe.

If one tries to restore, tentatively, a Sophoclean tragedy of four *epeisodia* divided by choral odes, such a sequence of events as sketched here will present itself as secured by Aristotle's mention of "the voice of the shuttle" as the means by which the Recognition in *Tereus* took place (*Poet.*, 16.1454b = Fr.595R). Since Aristotle takes the Recognition—by which he means "a change from ignorance to knowledge, producing love or hate between the persons destined by the poet for good or bad fortune" (*Poet.* 11.1452a)—to be central and of pivotal importance to a play, we may safely conclude that the Recognition in *Tereus* took place in the course of the action. What else can the Recognition be in this play than the discovery of Tereus' crime? It then follows that the crime was preceded by Procne's desire to receive a visit from her sister in the loneliness of her married life in a strange country (Frr.583R, 584R) and that a revenge exacted from Tereus by the women (Fr.589R) followed the Recognition, which occurred by means of "the voice of the shuttle," Fr.595R), with a triple metamorphosis added (Fr.581R). To fill the gaps in this rough plan of the play, we can avail ourselves of some 56 verses preserved from the original play, accounts and references by later writers and, for dramatic technique, parallels from extant plays. Accius' *Tereus* should also be referred to, since it is very likely to be a faithful translation of Sophocles' *Tereus*; for he had no other model to follow than Sophocles'.[37] His fidelity to Sophocles in translation by and large is defended.[38] Ovid, too, certainly knew and made use of Sophocles' *Tereus* in his *Metamorphoses* 6.422–676.[39] In presenting a tentative reconstruction of action, I shall describe the sequences, as if from the text. Of course, the possibility of different reconstructions remains open, but if this broad shape of action could be claimed with any degree of probability, that would give us a hint what the poet could have seen in this grim story of infanticide. (There will be no drastic difference from the versions presented by Welcker, Calder and Ribbeck [on Accius].)[40]

Dramatic time would be some four or five years after the marriage of Tereus and Procne (Frr.583R, 584R. The existence of a small child [Acc. Frr.652–53W] affirms the conjecture.)

Dramatic place would be before the palace of Tereus in Thrace (Fr.582R). Thucydides asserts vigorously that the event took place in Daulis, saying, "Teres, the father of Sitalces, was the first to establish the great kingdom of the Odrysians on a scale quite unknown to the rest of Thrace, a large portion of the Thracians being independent. This Teres is in no way related to Tereus, who married Pandion's daughter Procne from Athens; nor indeed did they belong to the same part of Thrace. Tereus lived in Daulis, part of what is now called Phocis, but which at that time was inhabited by Thracians. It was in this land that the women perpetrated the outrage upon Itys; and many of the poets when they mention the nightingale call it the Daulian bird."[41]

Thucydides' polemic is famous. Anything he finds "not reporting truth or facts" (1.21) he eagerly tries to correct. If he protests that many poets call a nightingale a Daulian bird and if such geographers as Pausanias and Strabo report to the same effect,[42] we must admit that the Daulian location was a traditional one and persisted long afterward. Thucydides' earnest protest must have been against Sophocles' version, which immediately after its presentation became the most prevalent.[43] Even if it was not an innovation, the Sophoclean location was evidently part of his dramatic design. Without doubt, he introduced the opposing themes of a civilized Athens and a barbarian Thrace.

Dramatis Personae, in Order of Appearance

Procne

In Fr.585R, she is directly addressed. Frr.583R and 584R are obviously words from the speech of Procne, who complains of the loneliness of her married life.

60

Nurse

Fr.583R is delivered to a confidante of Procne, presumably in the prologue. If the Chorus consisted of Thracian men, as will be shown next, a nurse, as in *Trachiniae*, would be the only suitable candidate.[44]

Chorus

Welcker and Calder thought that the Chorus were Thracian men. "Not merely do the philosophical sentiments of the preserved choral utterances (Frr.590R, 591R, 592R, 593R) suggest this. Procne, Ovid carefully tells us (*Met.* 6. 581–86), with remarkable control did not reveal her reaction to Philomela's message. She remained silent. The reason must be that she could not trust a hostile chorus (*cf.* Acc., Frr.643–44W), male retainers of her husband."[45]

Tereus

The title and Aristophanes, *Aves* 99 attest to his appearance.

Maid

Philomela, who has lost the power of speech, weaves her misfortune on a cloth. But if she is kept away from Procne, perhaps under custody, she needs an intermediary person to deliver this cloth. (Fr.588R could be an encouragement given to extract a hidden fact from a reluctant interlocutor.) Ovid (*Met.* 6.580) attests to a Thracian maid, who delivers unsuspectingly what she herself does not understand.

Philomela

Fr.589R testifies that the revenge done by the two sisters took place in the course of the action. A mutilated young woman, a miserable mute, would be indispensable concrete evidence of Tereus' savage deed.

Itys

Ovid attests to his appearance (*Met.* 6.620). He would be another mute.[46]

Messenger

"The triple metamorphosis could not take place on stage (Horace, *Ars* 187). A messenger is required to describe the miracle—as Theseus in *Oedipus Coloneus*."[47]

Deus ex machina

Fr.581R is spoken by one who can explain what happened and also foretell what will ensue. A mere human witness of the metamorphosis (*i.e.*, the messenger) cannot be the speaker. Welcker suggested Hermes as the deputy of Zeus,[48] who, I think, is more acceptable than Ares, suggested by Calder. Ares, a peculiarly Thracian god, with his close relationship with Dionysus and Aphrodite (see below, p. 79) and above all as the father of Tereus,[49] seems appropriate, but Fr.589R is most likely to be the final remark of the deity concerning the whole event (*cf.* note 76 on Fr.589R). The judgment is neutral, and the sentiment is genuinely Greek, recommending regulation, which sounds improbable in the mouth of a god whose basic characteristic is destructiveness. The phrase "Zeus commiserating" of the scholiast (Ar., *Av.* 212) suggests Zeus as the originator of the metamorphosis and Hermes as his messenger.

Tentative Reconstruction of the Action

Prologue

Sophocles preferred a conversational prologue to a Euripidean monologue.[50] Procne's lament about the loneliness of her secluded married life, including Fr.583R, would be delivered to the nurse, as in the prologue of *Trachiniae,* and would be properly placed here to open up the whole action.

Fr.583R.

νῦν δ' οὐδέν εἰμι χωρίς. ἀλλὰ πολλάκις
ἔβλεψα ταύτῃ τὴν γυναικείαν φύσιν,
ὡς οὐδέν ἐσμεν. αἱ νέαι μὲν ἐν πατρὸς
ἥδιστον, οἶμαι, ζῶμεν ἀνθρώπων βίον·
τερπνῶς γὰρ ἀεὶ παῖδας ἀνοία τρέφει.
ὅταν δ' ἐς ἥβην ἐξικώμεθ' ἔμφρονες,
ὠθούμεθ' ἔξω καὶ διεμπολώμεθα
θεῶν πατρῴων τῶν τε φυσάντων ἄπο,
αἱ μὲν ξένους πρὸς ἄνδρας, αἱ δὲ βαρβάρους,
αἱ δ' εἰς ἀήθη δώμαθ', αἱ δ' ἐπίρροθα.
καὶ ταῦτ', ἐπειδὰν εὐφρόνη ζεύξῃ μία,
χρεὼν ἐπαινεῖν καὶ δοκεῖν καλῶς ἔχειν

But now, separated from home, I am undone. Often, indeed, have I observed how miserable my sex is in this respect. When we are

63

girls, our life in our father's house is the sweetest, methinks, that can fall to mortals; for the days of thoughtless childhood are ever glad. But when we come to years of discretion, we are thrust out and sold in marriage far away from our ancestral gods and from our parents: some of us to other parts of Hellas, some to barbarians, some into houses where all is strange ($\dot{\alpha}\dot{\eta}\theta\eta$),[51] some into places of reproach. And in all this, when once the nuptial night is past, we must acquiesce, and deem that it is well.

Translation by R. C. Jebb

$\nu\bar{\upsilon}\nu$ δ' in the first line shows that the speech preceding this passage revealed something that had been contrary to the present state of lonely married life in an estranged house. Presumably the heroine's former life in the Athenian royal palace was recalled, with its distinguished ancient lineage, the glory and power of her father and ancestors. Fr.655W seems to be a part of an expository speech of how the fame of her father had spread even as far as this barbarous land so that Tereus rushed to join the battle that Pandion fought with the Labdacids (Apollod., *Bibl.* 3.14.8), and this was the reason why Tereus was rewarded with the king's daughter.

Fr.655W.
Famae nam nobilitas late ex stirpe praeclara evagat.
For fame's renown goes marching far and wide
If sprung from an illustrious stock.[52]

Happy memories rouse her yearning only after a reunion with her sister, who is enjoying merry, innocent days in an elegant Athenian palace. Fr.584R must be addressed to her at home.[53] Fr.584R:

$$\pi o \lambda \lambda \acute{\alpha} \ \sigma \varepsilon \ \zeta \eta \lambda \tilde{\omega} \ \beta \acute{\iota} o \upsilon,$$

$$\mu \acute{\alpha} \lambda \iota \sigma \tau \alpha \ \delta' \ \varepsilon \acute{\iota} \ \gamma \tilde{\eta} \varsigma \ \mu \grave{\eta} \ \pi \varepsilon \pi \varepsilon \acute{\iota} \rho \alpha \sigma \alpha \iota \ \xi \acute{\varepsilon} \nu \eta \varsigma$$

I envy you much for your life, especially if you have not experienced a strange land.

In dramatic economy, Sophocles must have been as efficient as in the prologue of *Oedipus Rex,* where Creon had already been despatched before the action had started. Procne must have asked Tereus to go to Athens and fetch Philomela before the play began, and his return is expected with great eagerness when the prologue ends. Frr.645–46W, here?:[54]

> *Atque id ego semper sic mecum agito et conparo*
> *quo pacto magnam molem minuam.*
>   This is the plan I ponder
> Making it ready ever in my mind—
> In what way I can lessen this large labor.

Parodus

The Chorus, consisting of Thracian elders, presumably appear to announce the king's return to the palace. Their constant presence on the stage helps to emphasize the loneliness of Procne.

First Episode

Tereus appears with a false report of Philomela's death —probably at sea.[55] Procne violently laments her loss. Fr.585R must be words of Tereus, who, hypocritically, consoles her.[56] Fr.585R:

> ἀλγεινά, Πρόκνη, δῆλον· ἀλλ᾽ ὅμως χρεὼν
> τὰ θεῖα θνητοὺς ὄντας εὐπετῶς φέρειν

No doubt it is harsh, Procne. But being mortals, we must accept and endure what is sent by the gods.

Procne erects a centoaph and provides funeral offerings (Ov., *Met.* 6.566–70) for a sister not dead, like Electra for a brother not dead.[57]

First Stasimon

During the recitation of this ode, one year of dramatic time passes, if we follow Ovid (*Met.* 6.571).[58]

Second Episode

Before Procne, who has not yet recovered from her sister's death, appears a maid with a gift of a *peplos*.[59] Philomela, after the rape by Tereus, was imprisoned, with her tongue cut out, in a mountain hut under the custody of a guard and a maid (*Met.* 6.572ff). The maid brings the *peplos*, as a gift traditionally dedicated to the queen at Dionysiac trieterica festivals, in which Philomela has woven her misfortune (*Met.* 6.587, cf. Fr.647W). Out of "the voice of the shuttle" is the rape "discovered," so Aristotle writes (*Poet.* 16.1454. b36ff = Fr.595R κερκίδος φωνή).

Some time would elapse before Procne was convinced of her sister's survival. She had long believed her to be dead. A maid with an ordinary gift would at first have met with indifference. She has difficulty in drawing the queen's attention to the *peplos*. Fr.587R:

φιλάργυρον μὲν πᾶν τὸ βάρβαρον γένος

Money-loving is all the barbarian race

66

may have been the reaction on Procne's side. But the queen's interest must have been aroused, and finally she even becomes inquisitive. Fr.588R would most appropriately be the words of Procne, who, awakening to the importance of the matter, now encourages the maid to reveal the facts. The maid, as described in Ovid, did not understand the message of the gift she herself had brought. When the queen suspects the truth and showers her with questions, the poor woman hesitates to speak. She fears punishment by Tereus. The queen encourages her. Fr.588R:

θάρσει· λέγων τἀληθὲς οὐ σφαλῇ ποτε

Have courage. Telling truth, you will never stumble.[60]

"The voice of the shuttle" was understood by Pearson to be a picture,[61] but that it was words was explicitly stated by Ovid (*Met.* 6.577, 582—*purpureae notae, carmen miserabile*), Apollodorus (*Bibl.* 3.14.8—γράμματα), the Scholiast (Ar., *Av.* 212. 6— διὰ γραμμάτων) and Libanius (*Narr.* 4.1103 1.17–18— γράμματα).

The impressive depiction by Ovid of the moment when Procne understands her sister's message was quoted above from Calder. The silence of a lady, conscious of her own high status, at a moment of deep sorrow is one of Sophocles' most successful psychological portraits (*cf.* Eurydice in *Antigone*, Jocasta in *Oedipus Rex*, Deianeira in *Trachiniae*). Ovid writes: "*carmen miserabile legit et (mirum potuisse) silet*" (*Met.* 6.582–83).[62]

The *epeisodion* must end with Procne's departure from the palace to go to her sister's prison. Ovid (587) says that she disguised herself as a Bacchant, left the palace, and joined the tumultuous crowd of the Bacchants. The excitement and freedom that the Dionysiac festival allowed women favored Procne.[63] Fr.647W will suit this sequence. The nurse may say this to Procne, or, more suitably, Procne may be talking to herself.[64]

67

Deum Cadmogena natum Semela adfare et famulanter pete.
Menialwise address and pray the god,
The son of Cadmus' daughter Semele.

"λίβανος, frankincense" (Fr.595aR), used also by Euripides in his description of Maenadism (*Bacch.* 144), could be a reference to the Dionysiac cult. Welcker (381) and Ribbeck (581) observe in Fr.586R that someone has caught sight of Procne hurrying out of the palace in a Maenad's attire.[65] I would rather accept Pearson's view that it is connected with the gift of the trieterica from Philomela. Because it is cited for a metrical peculiarity and not for sense, we cannot understand it satisfactorily, but Pearson supposes such a sequence, Fr.586R,:

σπεύδουσαν αὐτήν, ἐν δὲ ποικίλῳ φάρει

[I asked of her] what she was ready enough [to tell]; for on the embroidered robe . . .[66]

Second Stasimon

"A Dionysiac theme would be appropriate."[67] Fr.591R as cited below (p. 83) may be placed here.

Third Episode

The mutilated young woman must appear before the audience, a concrete picture of the outrageous crime of Tereus. Procne returns with Philomela in a Maenad's attire (Ov., *Met.* 6.601ff). On behalf of the tongueless victim, Procne tells the Chorus and the audience how the grotesque deed of Tereus was carried out from the very beginning. Frr.648–49W:

. . . *O suavem linguae sonitum o dulcitas
conspirantum animae!*

68

How pleasant is the sound of tongue that speaks!
O sweetness of their breath who breathe as one!

Frr.639–42W:

> *Tereus indomito more atque animo barbaro*
> *conspexit in eam; amore vecors flammeo,*
> *depositus, facinus pessimum ex dementia*
> *confingit.*
> Tereus, a man of ways untamable
> And savage heart, did turn his gaze upon her;
> Senseless with flaming love, a man laid low,
> The foulest deed he fashioned from his madness.

Ovid gives Procne a long, impassioned speech, scolding her
tearful sister while she herself is seething with rage (611ff): "This
is no time for tears, but for the sword, for something stronger
than the sword, if you have such a thing." While Procne was
thus speaking, Itys came into his mother's presence. His arrival
suggested what she could do, and regarding him with pitiless
eyes, she said, "Ah, how like your father you are!"[68] Philomela
is a voiceless, intimidated girl. She offsets the growing audacity
of Procne, who makes up her mind to commit infanticide. The
Chorus may not be told about the details of the revenge plan, but
they do not fail to realize the imminence of danger. There is
concern for the safety of Itys, possibly on the part of the nurse.
Frr.652–53W;

> *Set nisi clam regem auferre ab regina occupo*
> *puerum,*
> But if, the king unknowing, I do not
> Take from the queen the boy, forestalling her.

Third Stasimon

During this ode, Itys must be killed and cooked (Ov., *Met.*
6.642ff).

69

Fourth Episode

"Tereus enters, Procne seduces him into the palace with the pretext that she has prepared a sacred ancestral meal which he must consume alone (Ov., *Met.* 6.647ff). One recalls the carpet scene in Aeschylus, *Agamemnon.* The scene would conclude with the exit of Tereus and Procne into the central door of the *scaenae frons.*"[69] The Chorus by now may know, if not about the death of Itys, at least that something horrible is about to happen. Although they cannot help feeling sympathy for the wounded women, they are loyal to their king. They try to dissuade Procne. Frr.643–44W;

> *Video te, mulier, more multarum utier*
> *ut vim contendas tuam ad maiestatem viri.*
> I perceive you practice, woman,
> The ways of many wives, in that you strain
> Your might against your husband's dignity.

But an ominous reply silences them. Fr.650W:

> *Alia hic sanctitudo est, aliud nomen et numen*
> *Iovis.*
> Here holiness is different, different here
> The name and nod of Jupiter.

The Chorus, in spite of remaining critical of the sisters' awful revenge plan, eventually acquiesce and let it pass. Fr.651W:

> *Struunt sorores Atticae dirum nefas.*
> Dire wickedness the Attic sisters plot.

Fourth Stasimon

Tereus must have his meal during this ode. (Ov., *Met.* 6.650)

70

Someone (nurse?) appears from the *scaenae frons* and recounts in detail the murder of Itys, the preparation of the stew, the meal of Tereus, his discovery and rage and pursuit armed of the Athenian sisters. Ovid writes (650ff) that Tereus, unsuspecting, asks for his son, Itys. Procne answers, *"Intus habes, quem poscis."*

Fr.654W must be part of the report of how Philomela then sprang forward and hurled the head of Itys into Tereus' face (Ov., *Met.* 6.658–60).

> *Nova advena animo audaci in medium proripit sese*
> *ferox.*
> The strange newcomer, fierce and bold of heart,
> Thrusts herself forth into the midst.

Fr.582R must be Tereus' bitter cry on discovery of what he has eaten rather than Procne's address to the sun on her first appearance, as Buchwald conjectures.[70] Fr.582R:

''Ηλιε, φιλίπποις Θρῃξὶ πρέσβιστον σέλας[71]

O sun, the light most revered by the horse-loving Thracians!

Tereus' pursuit of the two Athenian women, perhaps reported by the nurse or a messenger, is mentioned by Aristophanes (*Lys.* 563)[72] as if the speech was impressive enough to be remembered by many members of the audience. Some vase-paintings, including those of later dates, may reflect it, as often the vases illustrated a messenger speech.[73] The miraculous triple metamorphosis will also be related.[74]

Fr.581R, which Aristotle cited as from Aeschylus, was correctly attributed by Welcker to a divine character in Sophocles' *Tereus*.[75]

τοῦτον δ᾿ ἐπόπτην ἔποπα τῶν αὑτοῦ κακῶν

πεποικίλωκε κἀποδηλώσας ἔχει

θρασὺν πετραῖον ὄρνιν ἐν παντευχίᾳ·

ὃς ἦρι μὲν φανέντι διαπαλεῖ πτερὸν

κίρκου λεπάργου· δύο γὰρ οὖν μορφὰς φανεῖ

παιδός τε χαὑτοῦ νηδύος μιᾶς ἄπο·

νέας δ᾿ ὀπώρας ἡνίκ᾿ ἂν ξανθῇ στάχυς,

στικτή νιν αὖθις ἀμφινωμήσει πτέρυξ·

ἀεὶ δὲ μίσει τῶνδ᾿ †ἀπ᾿ ἄλλον† εἰς τόπον

δρυμοὺς ἐρήμους καὶ πάγους ἀποικιεῖ

And this hoopoe, the spectator of his own misfortune, he (Zeus) has embroidered. He has manifested him as a bird bold, living among rocks, in full armor. When spring comes, it will ply the wing of a hawk with white feathers, for accordingly he will display two forms from a single womb, both the fledgling's and his own. Whenever the ear of corn grows yellow in early July, a spotted wing will guide him anew. But it will always fly away driven with hatred from these [women] to another place. He will inhabit lonely thickets and crags.

The divine character would have passed a final remark on the whole affair.[76] Fr.589R:

ἄνους ἐκεῖνος· αἱ δ᾿ ἀνουστέρως ἔτι

ἐκεῖνον ἠμύναντο ⟨πρὸς τὸ⟩ καρτερόν.

ὅστις γὰρ ἐν κακοῖσι θυμωθεὶς βροτῶν

μεῖζον προσάπτει τῆς νόσου τὸ φάρμακον,

ἰατρός ἐστιν οὐκ ἐπιστήμων κακῶν

He is foolish, but the women went, more foolishly too far in avenging him. For a person who, excited in misfortune, fixes on the remedy greater than the disease is a physician who does not understand misfortune.

The basic idea of the remark is that mortals should retain soundness, balance, and sanity of the mind in all circumstances—an idea that is typically Greek. The speaker, convicting the Thracian king and the Athenian princesses of a lack of reason, would most appropriately be a divine character, possibly Hermes conveying Zeus' judgment on the present case and general recommendation of regulation.

In Fr.590R Buchwald recognized a great resemblance to the closing words by the Chorus of the *Ajax* and *Trachiniae* in both idea and diction.[77] Fr.590R:

θνητὴν δὲ φύσιν χρὴ θνητὰ φρονεῖν,
τοῦτο κατειδότας ὡς οὐκ ἔστιν
πλὴν Διὸς οὐδεὶς τῶν μελλόντων
ταμίας ὅ τι χρὴ τετελέσθαι.

Men of mortal race must think mortal thoughts.
Knowing this full well, that there is none
But Zeus to dispose of what is to come
In the way that it must be accomplished.[78]

Frr.592R and 593R cannot be securely placed, but the sentiment is quite suitably understood as remarks commenting on a human level on what happened in the drama. Metrical similarity with *Oedipus Rex* and *Ajax* is pointed out by Buchwald.[79] Fr.592R:

ἀλλὰ τῶν πολλῶν καλῶν

τίς χάρις εἰ κακόβουλος

φροντὶς ἐκτρίψει τὸν εὐαίωνα πλοῦτον;

τὰν γὰρ ἀνθρώπου ζοὰν

ποικιλομήτιδες ἆται

πημάτων πάσαις μεταλλάσσουσιν ὥραις

What delight is there in many fair things,
if base brooding will destroy the blessed
wealth, root and branch?
For wily destruction bringing misfortunes
alter man's life at all seasons.

Fr.593R:

ζώοι τις ἀνθρώπων τὸ κατ' ἦμαρ ὅπως

ἥδιστα πορσύνων· τὸ δ' ἐς αὔριον αἰεὶ

τυφλὸν ἕρπει

Let a man live, being a man
    With brief dispose for the day,
As within that narrower span
    To enjoy what pleasure he may,
For the path is blind of the morrow
    And darkness wrappeth it round.[80]

3

The only undisputed evidence to place the play chronologically is that Aristophanes in *Aves* of 414 B.C. parodied Sophocles by letting Tereus appear as the king of the birds' empire (100).

Taking into account the performance of Philocles' *Pandionis,* which came after Sophocles and aroused Aristophanes' pointed remarks (see p. 57), 415 B.C. at least has to be precluded. However, a date well before 414 B.C. seems to be supported by the metrical similarity with *Ajax* and *Oedipus Rex* mentioned above, which points to an earlier production rather than the later or more mature years of the poet.[81]

Critics have discussed the chronology from its relationship with *Medea* and *Trachiniae.* Both *Medea* and *Tereus* depict wives taking vengeance upon faithless husbands by killing a child or children of their own. It is pointed out that in Tereus' story infanticide is central and indispensable because it is an aetiological part of the legend that tries to explain the voice of the nightingale, "Ityn, Ityn"; however, in the older Medean tale, the heroine merely absconds with her children, and the infanticide is a Euripidean innovation to the legend.[82] It is conjectured with much reason that he took it from *Tereus.*[83] But in *Medea* (1283) Procne is precluded from the instance of infanticide, whereas her deed is mentioned in *Hercules Furens* (1021) as "Procne's murder of her only child, (poeticized and) dedicated to the Muses."[84] In *Trachiniae,* a wife is also dishonored but she does not seek revenge; she tries to behave and to regain the lost love with a love charm. One may find these treatments of female psychology "Euripidean" and put *Trachiniae* and *Tereus* within the supposed period of Euripidean influence and its feedback.[85]

Dating it on the basis of the Atheno-Thracian antithesis is controversial.[86] The theme of the matrimonial ties between the two countries may suggest friendship, but the preposterous savagery of the Thracian king stimulates hostility. Archaeologists report that the Procne statue in the Acropolis Museum (dated to 430–20 B.C. by H. Knell[87]) may have been a dedication on the occasion of a victory in dramatic competition, possibly of Sophocles' *Tereus.*[88] If this furnishes external evidence for dating the play, it must be relatively early.

75

The discussion on chronology is inconclusive, but if the play was presented before the citizens when Athens was still in her most brilliant period, what was its effect on the audience? The choral ode of *Medea* proudly applauded Athenian glory on the eve of decay and the disruption of her empire (819–60). Probably the same audience saw the Athenian sisters' perpetration of unparalleled cruelties from which all human beings—nay, even beasts—would recoil. What was the intention of the poet in presenting such a story?

The answer may lie in one of the fragments. In Fr.589R, which is most certainly a final comment on the whole affair (Tereus' rape and mutilation of Philomela, the sisters' murder and cooking of Itys) given near the end of the play, not only is Tereus criticized as "thoughtless" but also Procne and Philomela as "more thoughtless." The terrible outrage perpetrated by the Athenian women is not vindicated as an inescapable result of a marriage with a barbarian and a life in alien surroundings. The Thracian king and the Athenian princesses are alike judged solely from the viewpoint of common human nature. The characters are put indiscriminately under the surveying light of Wisdom that exhorts all human beings to sobriety and moderation in times of misfortune. If the remark came from the mouth of a god, whose appearance can be safely conjectured from Fr.581R, the divine judgment would have reduced them all to pitiable victims of infatuation and indiscretion. An ending of a Sophoclean play with a *deus ex machina* is not frequent.[89] Here it would not have been a mere dramatic convenience. The mortals, looked down from above, convicted of a lack of reason, commiserated and ultimately inhumanized, the spectators cannot help feeling the diminution of human existence.

Both these features that Fr.589R seems to suggest—the common humanity of all men and the drama ending in a disintegration of human dignity—are what one would hardly expect of Sophocles if the preserved plays were all that bear witness to his capacity. Are they the mere arbitrary conceit of a modern reader or an overinterpretation of a fragment totally extraneous to the contents of the entire play? If the action of the play unfolded itself somewhat like the tentative reconstruction here presented, one would see how well the statement of Fr.589R, given in a dignified and powerful tone, confirms the whole drama.[90]

The point of the play, then, may be, phrased tentatively, that brutality in human nature, regardless of nationality, is veiled until it is disclosed in its sheer nakedness at a certain point in the action (Aristotle's Recognition (see p. 67)—the beginning of what I call here the third episode for the sake of reconstruction). There the Thracian king is revealed as a brute and the Athenian princess begins to show herself as a maddened beast. Tereus, by cutting out the tongue of his victim, and Procne, by cooking her son, both resorted to barbarism. But the play would not have started simply as a straight-forward exposure of bestiality in human nature nor as a clash between civilization and barbarism.

There was, doubtless, an emphasis on Greek civilized virtues in the initial characteristics of the women. Procne's speech (Fr.583R) in the opening scene testifies to intelligence in her accurate grasp of the situation and delicacy of the mind. She expressly calls her own people Greeks, differentiating βαρβάρους from ξένους. By Aristotle's testimonium, we know that the device of "the voice of the shuttle" (Fr.595R), by means of which Philomela informs her sister of her own survival and the crime of Tereus, was composed by Sophocles. Aristotle regards this sort of "discoveries composed by the poet" as "inartistic" and inferior to the "discovery brought about directly by the incidents" when he discusses the kinds of "discovery = recognition" from the viewpoint of dramatic technique (*Poet.* 16.1454.b.36ff). Sophocles is a master of the discovery of the latter kind. He could have put one in *Tereus* if he had wished. The discovery by means of "the voice of the shuttle" was obviously part of Sophocles' dramatic design. For knowledge of letters would be a sign of accomplished gentility when illiteracy was not uncommon.[91] That "the voice of the shuttle" means woven letters is easily guessed. Letters are symbols of civilized life. Weaving is also one of the basic arts of human culture and a skill to be admired in women. The resourceless victim of rape made a desperate bid for rescue in letters interwoven, possibly in a *peplos*. Inventiveness produced the means of communication for the mutilated girl.

If the refinement of the Athenian princesses were put to the forefront, would Tereus have entered as a typical barbarian in strong contrast to them? Herodotus characterized the Thracians as warlike (2.167, 4.94, 5.6) and cruel (4.94, 8.116). Sophocles would have made use of the information as effectively as he did in other plays. We cannot tell in what precise form Tereus was represented, whether as a fierce tyrant or an ugly erotomaniac.[92] But this middle-aged king of a savage tribe was certainly not a mere incarnation of bestiality in the first half of the play as reconstructed above. He at least had the intention of hiding his crime. Tereus lies (Ov., *Met.* 6.563–66), pretends innocence, and deceives his wife by manipulating words. (If my attribution of Fr.585R to Tereus in this scene is right, he is acting as a loving husband who tries to console his wife in her grief.) How the polygamous institution of a Thracian tribe also reported by Herodotus (5.5–6) could have been treated in this play is not known. But we must appreciate the sense of compunction or guilt of Tereus when we are told that he took measures lest his deed should be known to his wife [εὐλ]αβούμενος δὲ μὴ τῇ ἀ[δελφῇ μηνύσῃ ἐγλωσσοτόμη[σε τὴν παῖδα.] *(Hypothesis.)* He feels that he has trampled the inviolable relationship between man and wife.

A comparison with a parallel situation may throw some light on his character. Heracles in *Trachiniae* appears extremely rude and even brutal when he does not try to conceal to his wife his sexual desire for a young woman (480). He is not considerate and does not care to what torture he exposes Deianeira. He pays no attention to the purpose Deianeira had concealed with the

78

homicide she unintentionally committed (1137); deeds and results are all that matter to Heracles, as in any primitive society. In his world, the difference between reality and the way things appear to be, although one cardinal aspect of human life, is not worth giving thought to, as far as his relations with women are concerned. (Ironically enough, he belatedly finds out his failure on the brink of death, as often mentioned as an example of "late-learning" motif, conspicuous in Sophocles (*cf.* chapter 4, note 18). On the contrary, Tereus is aware that he has incestuously flouted kindred affection and ties.

We must assume that up to the end of the second episode of this tentative reconstruction, Procne and Tereus are a respectable king and queen. It would be only after a detailed account of Tereus' crime is somehow given (Frr.639–42W?, "the voice of the shuttle" must in some way be rendered into words intelligible to the audience) that their brutality could be revealed. Tereus would now be shown as a lascivious wolf that has overpowered an intimidated lamb (Ov., *Met.* 6.527–28). He has added to the degradation by cutting out the tongue of his prey, depriving her of speech.

There is no clue that might hint at the way that Procne would have allowed barbarism to take her over. The disclosure of Tereus' treachery (Fr.595R) may have been enough to perturb her passion and place her under the supremacy of the irrational. But to drive her to such an extreme of brutality, an additional incentive may be suspected. Ovid tells us that the Bacchic festival was used as an expedient for Procne to leave the palace in search of Philomela (*Met.* 6.590). The evidence for a Bacchic element (Fr.595aR, Fr.647W) is not perfectly conclusive. But the theme of sexual passion, which in Greek tradition would be represented by Aphrodite, operating as a disastrous power, could call for another god of emotional turbulence, Dionysus. Close association of Aphrodite and Dionysus in popular Greek thought is to be recognized in art and literature.[93] Sophocles' concern for the uncontrollable emotion, notably in the combination of Eros and Dionysus, is noticed in an ode of *Antigone*.[94] The location in Thrace also would have suggested Dionysus to the fifth-century audience.[95] It is precisely in this play where the action swirls along the edge of sobriety that Bacchism is to be brought in, and not merely as a dramatic expedient.[96]

A Dionysiac festival was a "liberation from the trammels and duties of civilized life (and so has a peculiar attraction for women of any age when their life is dull and their instincts repressed) from the limitations and responsibilities of individualities, from the burden of self-knowledge, from the effort of thought and from care for the past or the future."[97] The infectious enthusiasm in a congregational experience sweeps even the respectable away from their will. Once Procne has mingled herself with the crowd of the Maenadic turmoil, "shrill clashes of cymbals echoing in the mountain of Rhodope, wearing a deer skin with vines and a spear, shouting with other women that strange cry 'euhoi' " (Ov., *Met.* 6.587–600), she can easily shake off her indoor modesty and discretion. If she returns from the search for Philomela in a Maenad's attire, as told by Ovid, at the beginning of the third episode of the tentative reconstruction, the spectators would think it natural that a great change has taken place in Procne's soul during the time of her absence from the stage. (In Sophocles, the third episode often heralds a new turn in the action.[98]) If the description of Tereus' despicable deed (Frr.639–42W?) unmasks this lustful brute, her rage must grow to become a formidable mass of passion to let her take retaliatory measures.

In the fourth episode of the tentative reconstruction where, I suggested, an invitation to the infamous banquet would have been made, Procne must coax her husband to await the prepared meal. Now it would be her turn to conceal something—the horrendous butchery of their son (which must be completed in the third stasimon in my reconstruction)—with embellished words and flattery to the patriarchal authority by the name of which Tereus is entitled to have his feast alone (Ov., *Met.* 6.648). We cannot tell how much the Chorus knew, but the audience, who know the legend, would be able to see that the decorum, sophisticated tact of the temptation speech, and affected guise of a diligent wife as imaginable from Ovid (*Met.* 6.648) conceal the macabre bloodshed, the true nature of the prepared meal, and her expectant joy of serving the stew (*Met.* 6.653).

The messenger's (or the nurse's) account of the blasphemous meal (Exodus) would picture both Procne and the "strange newcomer, fierce and bold of heart thrusting herself forth into the midst" (Fr.654W) as more beastlike than beasts.

If the end of a play shapes the audience's final understanding, the report of the maddened pursuit of two women by a man who has eaten his own son (Ar., *Lys.* 563), their metamorphosis into birds and the divine revelation of what their future will be like, devoid of speech (Fr.581R), all jointly point to the diminution of human existence.

If we were not off the scent, the presupposed distinction between civilization and barbarism turned out to be fallacious. All the principal characters of the play allowed themselves to be carried away to the frontiers of humanity and brutality, placing the drama at the adjoining areas of civilization and barbarism. It is true that the Thracian king has acted like a barbarian by scoffing at the trust of the aged king, by not caring about the girl's virginity and his bonds of wedlock, but the Athenian princesses, too, have infringed upon human dignity by allowing the consumption of a child by the father. Neither the Athenian sisters nor the Thracian royalty could overpower the distresses of the ill-fated marriage.

It may be worthwhile to mention here that modern criticism has been split into two groups as to the problem of barbarism versus civilization in Euripides' *Medea*.[99] In *Medea,* to which *Tereus* constitutes an exact parallel with the theme of an unjustly treated wife and the conclusion of revenge by killing a child or children of their own, as indicated above in connection with chronology, the roles of civilized and barbarian characters are exchanged. The wronged wife is a barbarian, and the unfeeling husband is a Greek. Some scholars have asserted that the atrocious cruelty of infanticide committed by Medea is explained by her barbarian origin. If, on the contrary, one shares the view of the opposite side, the case may be stated as the following: Medea is presented from the start, despite her barbarian status, as a woman of high intelligence (285, 303) as well as of passionate temper (38, 446). Her intellect is demonstrated in the firm grip of her position (230ff), described with well-chosen words in her discourse, which shows a remarkable resemblance to that of Procne (Fr.583R). Forlorn and betrayed in a strange country, shorn of everything that might support and save her in her downfall, were she to possess the position of princess, intelligence and words are the only things left for her to exploit. She exerts all her intellectual power in forming an efficacious plan. In carrying it out, she never loses full command of her will and conscious control of herself. The firmness of her character and her absolute management of herself, her efficiency and gigantic effort in the fulfilment of her purpose, are so impressive and praiseworthy that, when at the end of the play she becomes an elevated being, inaccessible to Jason, a kind of God *ex machina*, [100] the audience accepts the tragic grandeur of her figure as a natural conclusion to the play. One can even say that Medea of Euripides, in her articulate speech and uninhibited action, is virtually Greek. [101] Her self-reliance is what the Athenian would value in his fellow citizen. If such a view is found to be sound, which I believe it to be, one may reasonably say that a dramatist can create a tragic hero out of a barbarian and a barbarian out of a civilized character. Criticism can also shift round from one position to another. As the interpretation of Creon in *Antigone* and Medea in *Medea* has formed two opposing parties, so in other plays one character can be met with two different views. It would be no wonder if some plays of Sophocles had had two different groups of supporters, the one more enthusiastic and the other less ardent, and, Fortune failing to favor the former, had not survived into the later centuries.

Whatever the circumstances were, the fact is that the concept of the single origin and nature of mankind becomes prominent in the closing decades of the fifth century B.C., especially through the voices and activities of sophists and physicians.[102] Sophocles would not have held himself aloof from the contemporary tide of thought. It has been suggested that Fr.591R echoes the principle of the equality of human beings, which is a basic idea of Dionysiac religion.[103]

> ἓν φῦλον ἀνθρώπων, μί' ἔδειξε πατρὸς
>
> καὶ ματρὸς ἡμᾶς ἁμέρα τοὺς πάντας· οὐδεὶς
>
> ἔξοχος ἄλλος ἔβλαστεν ἄλλου.
>
> βόσκει δὲ τοὺς μὲν μοῖρα δυσαμερίας,
>
> τοὺς δ' ὄλβος ἡμῶν, τοὺς δὲ δουλεί-
>
> ας ζυγὸν ἔσχεν ἀνάγκας.

We are one from father and mother,
All human children of earth;
Not one more high than another,
Or lower babe at his birth:
But the daily food of his living
Is that which Destiny gave;
And Weal or Woe is her giving,
Or hardest yoke of the slave.

We do not know in what detail Sophocles inserted this Dionysiac doctrine into the gruesome story of infanticide and cannibalism, but this explicit statement of the common humanity of all men would have been the underlying theme of the play.

Might one expect of a "classical, purely Greek poet" such a play, testimony, most probably, to absolute open-mindedness? The sentiments expressed in some fragments, supported by what the tentative reconstruction of the action suggests, seem to tell us that the poet was by no means indifferent to what we usually do not associate with Sophocles: a positively fair attitude towards barbarians and concerns about the power of the irrational in the sexual area of human nature. It seems that the play was liked by the audiences of the fifth and fourth centuries B.C.[104] but was not chosen by the "selector." We can well imagine that the fourth-century audiences who liked Euripides found in *Tereus* something that appealed to their senses and sensibilities—men and women not as conquerors but as victims of their own blind inner urges, while the "selector" found it un-Sophoclean.

However, if we are led to suppose that Sophocles did make a tragic character of an infatuated middle-aged woman, not only of an unyielding, high-minded maiden, as in the existing drama, that Sophocles did end his play in human defeat and not only in victory as in our preserved plays, we may reasonably reconsider the seven "selected" plays in a wider context of what might be provisionally called Sophoclean liberalism, and not be satisfied by evaluating them only from the viewpoint of Sophoclean tragic heroism.

We shall resume the second topic, which my chapter on *Tereus* gives rise to, Sophocles and the irrational, in chapter 5. For the subject of chapter 4, we shall have *Philoctetes*, the only precisely dated "selected" play. The play is put next to the last in the chronological order of Sophocles' extant works and must tell us about the aged poet's view of life after he has seen the world and learned the minds of people.

The play must tell us, above all, about the old Sophocles' idea of tragic heroism, as it stands in significant contrast to *Ajax*, the earliest extant play in which we saw that quintessence of Sophoclean poetry shaped, at least partly, from the traditional pattern of theomachy and widened into an ethical vision to be passed intact to succeeding Sophoclean heroes. Our concern throughout the chapters has been whether the poet has held the same ideal of tragic heroism, always, in all his works, whether his lofty-minded hero is to be left isolated in eternal loneliness, "hated by the gods and nature" (*Aj.* 459).

The most prominent characteristics of the central characters of *Ajax* and *Philoctetes* may be phrased, in the same words, as rigidity, refusal to compromise, and godliness. But between the two plays there is all the difference in the world in one point: the hero changes his mind in *Philoctetes*. Now that we have had a brief survey over two lost plays and glimpsed the possibility of "un-Sophoclean" features, including a possible change of heart of a hero, we may review this next-to-last extant play under the light that has directed our eyes to what may have been left eclipsed by the towering grandeur of the surviving heroes.

In reconsidering *Philoctetes*, therefore, we will stand on the opposite side of its hero and his heroism; we will have Odysseus as the subject of our discussion. Odysseus plays an important part in *Philoctetes*, important in the sense that the whole action of the play is concerned with his attempt to take out Philoctetes to Troy. He professes that he works for the benefit of the whole Greek army. This would make him represent his community, just as he did in a different way in *Ajax*. Odysseus, appearing as a "fixer" in both *Ajax* and *Philoctetes*, would urge us to be watchful about the poet's handling of society in its relationship to the hero.

Odysseus' appearance in *Philoctetes* is also important in the sense that he is often supposed to be equipped with propensities diametrically opposed to those of Sophoclean heroes: quick to change, ready to compromise, full of clever tactics. There is a widespread assumption that Odysseus in *Philoctetes* is one of the most detestable characters Sophocles has depicted, made to set off the noble and lofty heroism of Philoctetes.

85

It is worth considering if that is true. Odysseus appeared in other Sophoclean plays fairly often, although the loss of the great majority of the evidence does not allow us to know how. Odysseus was one of the most popular figures in Greek myths, sung about by poets and loved by people. How did Sophocles estimate the Odyssean qualities that seem to contradict the poet's idea of tragic heroism?

4.

Sophocles and Odysseus

1

It is no accident that Sophocles called upon Odysseus in many of his plays.[1] In mythical tradition, Odysseus' chief virtue is intelligence, and words and speech are its direct expression. Sophocles, who is said to have introduced the third actor to the Greek theatre,[2] must have been particularly keen to explore the capacity of dramatic speeches.

In the gallant world of the *Iliad,* where physical force and bravery in battle dominate, the range for Odysseus' activities is comparatively limited, although the important roles he plays as a diplomat, an orator, and an arbiter should not be underrated.[3] The *Odyssey* gives the hero ample opportunities to exert his wits and his talent for conversation. He "saw many towns of many people, learned their minds and suffered many woes in his heart" (*Od.* 1.1–4), so he knows humanity; he knows how to talk to people. One would be reminded how his attractive manner of speech arouses gentle feelings in a princess, sincere loyalty in his servants, and deep love in his wife. His comments on various occasions, his lies and tricks on words, are perfect. They save himself, his family, and his comrades in the perils of seafaring and homecoming. It is in the *Odyssey* that Odysseus is characterized as a hero of *polymetis* (abounding in ideas) and *polytlas* (much-enduring), a favorite with people of all ages, in all ages.

During the centuries after Homer, Odysseus' image as an affectionate family man, a skillful sailor, or a distinguished warrior with both wisdom and valor may have gone through changes.

In Cyclic epics, of which we have only fragmentary knowledge, he seems to make a great contribution to the Greek army in their fight against the Trojans. Indeed, it is more often Odysseus' wits and wiles that deliver the soldiers from danger and promote the common good than Achilles' pride, Ajax's magnanimity, or the virtues of other loftier generals. But Odysseus' trickery and opportunistic creed at times applied in equivocal methods were sufficient reason to provoke moralistic controversy. No other hero was so heartily detested by Pindar, that invincible upholder of aristocracy.[4]

Sophocles, as a citizen of democratic Athens, himself engaged in important political offices, must have appreciated the virtues of Odysseus, who could persuade, mediate, negotiate, and settle problems. Sophocles, as a dramatist, must have seen the possibilities of Odysseus, not only as a proficient speaker to help the action develop but also to introduce innovations away from the well-beaten track of legend. Both in title roles and as a pivotal character, Sophocles used him throughout the years of his play-writing, from early *Nausicaa*[5] to late *Philoctetes*.

In *Ajax,* contrasting with Ajax's self-centered monumental rigidity by which he is strictly tied to an aristocratic sense of honor, Odysseus' flexibility is dramatically explored to shape itself into philanthropic codes of democracy. Unlike Ajax, who was hostile to human society as well as to the gods, Odysseus attests to his piety by accepting the gods' ordinance, under which all mortals are to live together. His tolerance and generosity enable him to persuade others (1373) and be persuaded by others (1400) to bring the action of the play to an end. The tragic glory of the heroic past, symbolized by Ajax's death, is balanced by Odysseus' heralding of the age of the common. He sews up the wound left gaping by the self-murder of the noble but stubborn hero. Odysseus, representing the society of equals and blessed by Athena (132),[6] the coming future is also blessed.

If we turn our eyes to the lost plays, we find only a few fragments left from *Odysseus Mainomenos,* but its contents are divined from the title itself.[7] Odysseus' pretended insanity employed to avoid the obligation of joining the Trojan expedition is detected by Palamedes' ruse. As Odysseus was plowing with a horse and an ox yoked together to feign madness, Palamedes put Odysseus' son before the plow. Odysseus stopped it, and his sham madness was disclosed. No evidence is left for the reason in Sophocles' play of Odysseus' reluctance to take part in the Trojan expedition. But the basic assumption for the character of Odysseus in this play would be, as in Homeric tradition, that he was primarily a farmer owing an estate. He loved his land as much as his people. We do not know what the play was like, but, as in the *Odyssey,* the farmer becomes a sailor, compelled by necessity, so in this play a son-loving father becomes, in all probability, a man-killing soldier, bound by an oath.

Taking up the story of Agamemnon's quandary in Aulis, in which the feigned betrothal of Iphigenia to Achilles had been the traditional theme,[8] Sophocles in his *Iphigenia in Aulis* made Odysseus pretend to be on a beneficial mission, addressing Clytaemnestra thus:

O you obtained the greatest son-in-law! (Fr.305R).

Evidently Odysseus is trying to rescue the Greek army becalmed in Aulis by the wrath of Artemis, for the appeasement of which a virgin ought to be sacrificed. We do not know if he tried to justify his fraud by the cause of public good, as he did in *Philoctetes* (see p. 100), but its merciless execution would have aroused ethical protest in one form or another.[9] According to the literary tradition, the deceit works well, Iphigenia is sacrificed, and the Greeks can set sail.

In *Syndeipnoi,* Odysseus urges Achilles, with a clever appeal to his youthful pride and self-respect, to give up his sulking (Fr.566R and probably Fr.564R). He is accused of being "capable of every [evil] thing" (Fr.567) on account of his slyness. No doubt Odysseus is acting for the common good of the fighting Greeks, although we do not know under what circumstances. In *Lacaenae,* Odysseus ventures to risk his life on behalf of the whole Greek army. In Fr.367R, he (or Diomedes) relates how he entered the city of Troy through a sewer. The purpose of this dangerous adventure was to get hold of the Palladium, possession of which was essential to the capture of Troy. The subject of *Scyrioi* is generally considered to be the summons of Neoptolemus from Scyrus by Odysseus and Phoenix, but nothing further is ascertainable.[10]

Odysseus wreaks atrocious vengeance upon his mortal enemy in *Palamedes.* Servius (ad *Aen.* 2.81), whom Robert, Wüst, and Stössl thought derived material from the Sophoclean version,[11] gives another incident that led Odysseus to carry out a most hideous plan of revenge. During the expedition Odysseus is sent to Thrace for a supply of provisions but returns empty-handed, whereas Palamedes brings back plenty. The first step to avenge himself of the double insult on his sagacity was taken by Odysseus: he forged a letter addressed to Palamedes, which purported to be from Priam the Trojan king and expressed gratitude for Palamedes' treason, reporting a secret despatch of gold as a reward. Odysseus sent off a Phrygian captive with the letter and had him killed not far from the Greek camp. The letter was discovered and brought to Agamemnon, and read aloud before the assembled generals. They all accused Palamedes of being a traitor, but Odysseus, pretending to support him, proposed to search for gold to find out if the story was true. Odysseus had had gold buried by his slaves in the area of Palamedes' tent the previous night. The gold discovered, Palamedes was stoned to death.

Stössl acutely saw in Servius' words[12] *Tunc Ulixes cum se Palamedi adesse simularet, ait* a reflection of a scene where Odysseus "pretended to make a plea for Palamedes" and thought that Fr.479R was a part of his false defence speech:

> Did not this man stop their starvation? With reverence be it spoken. Did he not find, for those who after the painful struggle with whirling surges were taking rest,[13] draughts and dice, a most clever pastime that gives delight to the heart, a remedy for idleness?

If Stössl was right and if this tactful vindication speech had the effect of setting all the Achaean generals decisively against their savior in the end, leading to his murder according to the story, we would have had an Odysseus whose extraordinary eloquence and rhetorical skill could move, convince, and convert even old companions into entering upon a course of murderous vengeance.[14]

In *Teucer,* where Teucer's return to Salamis is probably the subject, Odysseus, though he does not traditionally belong to this story, appears and engages in an altercation, which Aristotle cites as an illustration of cogent argument.[15] It is undeniable that he played a great part in the sequence in which presumably Telamon's anger at the loss of Ajax and Eurysaces (Fr.577R) resulted in Teucer's departure for Cyprus.[16]

We cannot overlook the fact that Sophocles treated the death of Odysseus at odds with an oracle (Frr.460R, 461R). There is the difficult question of whether *Odysseus Acanthoplex* and *Niptra* are different titles for the same play (which seems very unlikely in a poet who is said to have followed the Homeric narrative as closely as possible).[17] In any case, Sophocles brought Odysseus onstage, awakening, on the brink of death (Cic., *Tusc. disp.* 2.48), to the real meaning of a Dodonan oracle, which, without seeming to, had prophesied the end of his life.[18] He had misinterpreted it and had safeguarded himself against his legitimate son instead of his bastard son. Consequently, Odysseus was mortally wounded by Telegonus. He acted at cross-purposes and learned the truth too late. The evidence is too meager to allow any substantial discussion, but it demands our attention that Sophocles treated Odysseus, who could have been, in one play or another, an odious impostor or a sophist competent enough to provide solutions to secular problems, coming to grips with a religious issue with a personal stake in it. Had the play remained intact, we should have seen another important phase of Sophocles' mind in touch with the soul of this untypical hero. It is easily seen that Sophocles used this versatile person not simply because of technical exigencies but because he had a genuine interest in his personality.[19]

2

Sophocles, in 409 B.C., near the end of his long and successful life as a dramatist, presented *Philoctetes*, the subject of which is the fetching of Philoctetes to Troy by Odysseus and Neoptolemus.

The drama begins with Odysseus, who has just arrived in Lemnos to take Philoctetes back to Troy in order to bring victory to the Greeks. It was Odysseus who had marooned him while seriously sick ten years before "by the order of the generals and for the profit of the whole army" (6, 10). Philoctetes will shoot him on sight with the bow he received from Heracles. The only possible way to take him out is by cunning, since no force or persuasion would work (101–103). Odysseus uses a young man as his instrument. Neoptolemus, the son of Achilles, abhors deceit by nature but is desirous of military acclaim. His father had been the first and foremost warrior in the Trojan field, and the son naturally aims at a fame worthy of his parentage. After a short display of reluctance on the part of the youth to obey his sharp-witted superior, the audience is made to understand that this susceptible young man is going to deceive with a false story the sick hero who has been left cruelly abandoned for ten years and is now badly needed for the conquest of Troy (—122).

The Chorus, sailors of Neoptolemus, are also committed to the trick and actively play their part. This makes the action extremely meaningful, as recent critics have elucidated.[20] The audience become most anxious to know how the intrigue will work out, how well Neoptolemus will carry out the plan, whether he will flinch out of pity and shame at the sight of the rugged, forlorn invalid, the awe-inspiring bow, the agonizing suffering, and the guileless personality of Philoctetes. The audience is not told in precise terms whether Philoctetes or the bow is wanted, or both, or how much Neoptolemus is informed about these points. The fluctuation of Neoptolemus' youthful mind on one hand (even as early as 230, at the beginning of the encounter, Neoptolemus stops, stunned by the miserable limping figure of Philoctetes, and falls silent for a while), on the other hand an unbelievably assured touch in performing the ruse (the virtuoso narrator giving such a vivid and minute report of a fictitious event (343–390) indeed outdoes his master) make the whole action peculiarly problematic. Each moment the audience is left uncertain whether Neoptolemus' conduct is sincere or simulated. Philoctetes' open-mindedness, even to the extent of gullibility (530, 628, 658ff), makes the matter all the more complex, as Odysseus' initial announcement of an execution of a ruse comes back to the audience's memory. The spectators are incessantly forced to suspend their judgment about what is really happening.[21] From time to time, the progress of the action seems to be delayed or jeopardized by hesitation, disbelief, or anger of the young man and the hero. The situation might turn about at any moment.

The last scene of friendly persuasion enacted by the repentant Neoptolemus again arouses in the audience's minds the tantalizing sense of contradiction and frustration. The admirable deed of Neoptolemus' self-sacrifice and the joint departure for Malis, Philoctetes' home country (1402–1408), which the audience think an understandable conclusion for this noble-hearted youth and the hero, still leave them unhappy as to which direction the action is taking. Has Neoptolemus given way under Philoctetes' intractability, and run out of patience (1402–)?[22] It seemed a moment ago that Neoptolemus' honesty had been trusted (1305—). In agreement with heaven's will, he argued the interests of Philoctetes convincingly, the promise of cure and glory awaiting him in Troy (1333–1335). But the dramatist goes out of his way to insert one line of Philoctetes' question that might bring the matter back to its start, "Why do you obey the Atreidae?" (1386) Neoptolemus does not answer straightforwardly (1387). He blames Philoctetes for his stubbornness. When Philoctetes refuses forever to go to Troy (1392), has he become no longer accessible? The words of Neoptolemus are enigmatic: "It seems best for me to abstain from *words*" (1395).[23] If this means dissociation, as it appears to do, followed by "best for you to live as you have so far done without salvation" (1396), how can Neoptolemus so readily consent to a return to Greece (1402)? Why is he so timidly and selfishly worried about the possible revenge on himself by the Achaeans (1404) which mars his otherwise impeccable chivalry? Why is this ambiguity even deeper than before when spirited *antilabae* suggest that the scene is approaching its end (1402–8)?[24] But the audience may assume from the trochaic tetrameter (1402–1408) that this is a provisional ending to be followed by an ultimate one.[25] The sustained obscurity of this double ending is thus obviously meant for the audience to perceive.

Nevertheless, what a relief that Neoptolemus has proved to be Achilles' noble son, at least to Philoctetes! How the hero rejoices to see his integrity respected! Easterling has pointed out the striking impression of lucidity of this play, attributing it largely to "psychological sureness of touch on the part of the poet.''[26] The writer's concentration on the immediate action is so great, his portrayal of the reactions of the characters so convincing, that each consecutive scene offers an immensely clear picture of how the characters respond. The spectators' attention is tightly arrested by the vividness of the moments; they feel themselves to be quite sure of the situation, but their most intense anticipations are disappointed.

This is exactly how we get in touch with reality. When we are caught in a situation not altogether simple and clear, we assume that the scenes we have witnessed, the words we have heard through our own ears give us the surest guarantee for believing the reality of what we have been in touch with. However, when a totally unexpected situation ensues (and this can happen pretty often in real life, not necessarily because somebody has been cheating as in this play), the discrepancy between what we believe to be real and what *is* real is so great that we can no longer trust our own understanding, no longer hold a consistent and coherent picture of the immediate past. What we actually witnessed could have been only appearance and simulation of what was really going on.

A large part of this complication rests on the fact that the words uttered, carefully or gratuitously, the speeches given with various human factors—hope and despair, trust and distrust, affection and hatred and so on—are imperfect and delusive in the basic qualities of their nature. The same word can mean different things to different people. Different people can speak differently of the same thing. Each individual sees things differently, and we fail to grasp the others' outlook. Partial knowledge is unsuspectingly taken for granted as a bird's-eye view. An essential aspect of a matter emerges from the shadows; late revelation clarifies earlier events.

What we experience as we watch *Philoctetes* in the tension of being kept in a state of suspended uncertainty, of being dahsed down from surface lucidity to ambiguity underneath is precisely what we have in our senses and minds, when we get in touch, in real life, with things and people through words and speeches. Sophocles has created here an exquisite dramatic version of reality that man can grasp only insufficiently through words and speeches, deceptiveness being the fundamental aspect of their nature.

In editing such an elaborate presentation of reality, Odysseus is adroitly used with a multishaded character portrayal of the traditional schemer. As long as he is onstage, he represents the extremely clear-cut figure of a man of action. In the opening scene, he acts efficiently, devoting heart and soul to his mission. He gives an apt and opposite description of the situation past and present, brief but right to the point, "wasting no time in long speech" (12). Complications start when he exits after having given his instruction of deceit to Neoptolemus (54–132). The young man has been told to steal Philoctetes' mind (55) by telling a false story of the wrongs done to him in Troy, and the youth sets to the work.

The story of Neoptolemus (343–90) is presented as a fabrication (55–57).[27] However, his description has such a ring of truth and his speech is so engaging that the audience cannot help doubting if the story is not entirely false. Odysseus is first pictured as "godlike Odysseus,"[28] coming to Scyrus, Neoptolemus' home country, "in a galley gaily decked" (344) with an invitation to a glorious future. He is a joyous messenger from the Greek army in Troy, which needs and welcomes the young man as a hope for victory (–358). Neoptolemus then proceeds to tell about his surprise and anger on his discovery of the assignment of his father's arms to Odysseus, how he emotionally protested ("I boiled with rage, I hurled at him abuse the bitterest tongue could frame" [374–75]) and how Odysseus, "though not prone to wrath . . . stung to the quick by my retort, replied, You were not here with us, but absent from your duty!" (377–79). The graphic depiction of himself and of Odysseus with their own words quoted in direct speeches assures Philoctetes and the audience how indignant he now is against Odysseus, the hero's mortal enemy. However, the story may be a downright lie in spite of "the ring of truth," and the fact that Odysseus is the ultimate author of the machination makes the matter doubly complex.

The false merchant's scene (542–627) contrasts with Neoptolemus' "story" picturing Odysseus as an "archfiend" who has come to wheedle Philoctetes to board his ship "to make a show of him to the Greek host" (622–30), but again by a crooked trick enacted by a dubious character.[29]

Ostensibly, the merchant is sent by Odysseus to help Neoptolemus when there was too much delay in carrying out the operations (126–31). As a matter of fact, he appears when Philoctetes is already duped and is about to set out for the ship. He gives a detailed report, indeed too detailed for the alleged purpose, on the capture of the Trojan prophet Helenus and Odysseus' ostentatious declaration to bring back Philoctetes by any means.

Probably because they include the crucial point that Philoctetes himself is required by the oracle, and not only the bow, and that he must be willing to go to Troy (612–13), the merchant's words have been taken seriously by critics, who after a meticulous study of the text can be safely sure of their relevance to the major issue. But the audience and Neoptolemus, who are not meant to believe the speech (130) but are not sure whether the merchant is acting as he was told or on his own behalf, would receive each word with suspicion and distrust, since the story has been declared untrue, and they know the speaker is masquerading and that a crafty manipulator is behind it. At the same time, the remarkable accuracy of description, with each little detail perfected, gives such a vivid picture of an event in a remote place that the audience finds it hard to brush it aside as a mere fiction. The more bizarre the picture of Odysseus, the less reliable the bogus speech sounds, but the more graphically lifelike it seems, the greater actuality it acquires. The words of the merchant are deliberately derogatory:

> whom (Helenus) this man, going forth by night—this guileful Odysseus, of whom all shameful and dishonouring words are spoken—made his prisoner; and, leading him in bonds, showed him publicly to the Achaeans, a goodly prize: who then prophesied to them whatso else they asked, and that they should never sack the towers of Troy, unless by winning words they should bring this man from the island whereon he now dwells.
>
> And the son of Laertes, when he heard the seer speak thus, straightway promised that he would bring this man and show him to the Achaeans—most likely, he thought, as a willing captive—but, if reluctant, then by force; adding that, should he fail in this, whoso wished might have his head.[30]

(606–19)

The main purpose of this fraudulent speech is that "this individual scene," like others, will "contribute to a totality of dramatic design"[31] of this play where the deceptiveness of human speech and the elusiveness of reality are part of the chief issue. But the speech also focuses the audience's attention upon Odysseus. It shows him as an eccentric credit-seeker, scrambling for distinction. Has Odysseus ventured on this dangerous but sweetly rewarding task driven by a thirst for fame? Has the merchant's story eventually brought us close to the truth of the matter, although it is presented as a fabrication in precisely the manner in which Neoptolemus' false story was told?

The two stories, both directed by Odysseus but told by characters in different positions, seem to complement one another remarkably well; while the groveling merchant pictures Odysseus in a scene characteristic of his strong bent towards success and glory, the youth "noble by nature" brings him to our minds' eye as an exemplary soldier performing his duty, self-denying in an almost servile obedience to the tyrannical scheme of the Atreidae. The indignant words of Odysseus, who seldom gets furious (καίπερ οὐ δύσοργος ὤν, 377) convey his exasperation with the boy, who, arriving late, claims respect as his privilege. The audience knew from the previous utterance of Odysseus (72–74) and knowledge of traditional myth that Odysseus had not been willing to participate in the Trojan expedition at first (*e.g.*, *Odysseus Mainomenos*, mentioned above). Despite that initial reluctance, once he has joined the army, he has suppressed his private complaints and accepted the prevailing order of the Atreidae (δεδώκασ᾽ ἐνδίκως οὗτοι τάδε· 372). Repressive discipline, self-effacement, and obedience to one's superiors are essential to a militaristic regime. The criticism of the young man's blustering boasts betrays Odysseus' deep regret for the waywardness of a young soldier. But the story may be a lie out of the whole truth.

The dramatist carefully keeps open the question whether these "stories" could be not altogether false, whether Odysseus could really have acted like that in the Greek camp at Troy. The audience find themselves trying to build up a coherent picture of this enigmatic man by adding up his images offered by two contrasting characters, a "noble" youth and a puzzling false-trader. Their curiosity is excited even more strongly, as they expect his reemergence on stage at the apparent failure of Neoptolemus' work (915–). When Odysseus appears next (974) and declares, at Philoctetes' resolute refusal to depart for Troy, "let him stay," but without the bow (1054–1056), his words have such compelling clarity on the surface, yet are so hard to penetrate that the same question obtrudes in our minds; what are we to make of his intervention? Does he mean what he says? Has he given up Philoctetes and thinks the capture of the bow to be enough? Or should we recognize the resourceful Odysseus quickly shifting to a new strategem of bluff?

His laconic reticence in this play has been pointed out by Ronnet.[32] The man famous for his readiness of speech and a glib tongue does not engage in a long argument in which he might have presented his case brilliantly.[33] What marks the vocabulary of this man of action in this sequence is an inescapable sameness of reiterated, ineffectual watchwords uttered in a futile attempt to frighten the youth and Philocotetes: Zeus' intention, the profit of the Achaeans, and the command of the Atreidae are the supreme cause for which he works and what the Greek soldiers must also serve unquestioningly. (Zeus' name is repeated with striking frequency three times in two lines (989–90), the Achaean cause is recurringly phrased as Achaeans, Argives, and the whole army, 67, 1243, 1250, 1257, 1294, and the Atreidae, 1294.) When he refers to his mission, facing Philoctetes, his speech tends to use verbal adjectives and future tenses, pointing to the future course aimed at by the collective will of the army or the multitude (981–83, 993, 994, 998, 1003). Odysseus, with this impersonal mode of expression and relative lack of eloquence, stands in patent contrast to the indignant Philoctetes, who pours out his personal rancor in a great profusion of words. We hear from Odysseus' mouth no discourse on the motives for his deeds (except for the very brief but accurate epitomization of his general moral code [1049–52]) or the personal and private sentiments in pursuing this dirty business of the fetching of Philoctetes. Instead, two long "made-up" stories of his behavior in the past, presented by a "noble-hearted" youth and by a dubious "feigned merchant," the one superimposed upon the other and further elaborated through vividness and remoteness at one time, could reveal his personal sentiments under an extremely ambiguous light. The deliberate equivocation through two extensive speeches of falsehood is followed by another sequence to multiply complications, and they all work together to compel the audience to suspend their judgment on Odysseus' identity.

By blotting the identity of Odysseus, the dramatist has also equivocated his mission. Since the false merchant is known to be giving a bogus speech, of which the ultimate manipulator is

Odysseus, the audience is left free to disbelieve his report. In fact, the devious words of the merchant color the oracle, of which the audience are informed in detail for the first time in the play, with a tint of discredit and unreality; the man who volunteers to follow out the difficult discretions of the oracle is revealed, most vividly but not without a sort of theatrical exaggeration, as a vainglorious exhibitionist. Yet Odysseus himself is here in Lemnos professing that he is a delegate of the Greeks who, convinced by the divine will, desperately want Philoctetes to come to Troy. Everyone in the audience is given a different range of choice in understanding the summons of Philoctetes: it can be a sacred public cause; it can also be taken as matter of conferring another prize on the careerist.

But the dramatic characters must make up their minds. As a promised savior of Greece, Neoptolemus is vividly conscious of his own position (114).[34] His quest for the means of its fulfilment exposes him to the constant danger of being swept off his feet by Odyssean logic (116).[35] Is he to obey his master simply as a junior soldier who is following an experienced superior? Or is he to act by his own code as a well-born man? But what if his distrust and disobedience cause offence to the Greeks?

Neoptolemus' difficulty is tied to Philoctetes' as the personal relationship grows between them. Suddenly dragged out of ten years' brooding over his resentment against his former comrades, who had pitilessly marooned him before and now try to recover him for their own ends, Philoctetes finds himself caught in a web of a more infuriating knavery of deceit and impudence. Although his love for Greece and loyalty to his countrymen is deep-rooted (223–24, 234, his concern about other generals 332, 410ff), he would deem himself rid of his sickness, if he could see Odysseus and the Atreidae destroyed (1043–44). It is not without much ado that he comes to be assured of seeing Achilles' noble son in Neoptolemus (1312). Finally, his hatred of the Atreidae and Odysseus, his anger against the evil and injustice they represent, overwhelms him, and the hero rejects the Trojan battlefield as no place for men of principles. But his affection and gratitude to the youth who has repented his part in the enterprise of the leaders almost shakes him from his decision (1350, 1352).

No one among the spectators of 409 B.C. would have watched the play as an event of the long-past Homeric Age where society, even the army, seemed to have been loosely organized and each individual hero could have acted by his own code of ethics. The bewilderment of Neoptolemus facing the mission imposed upon him, the agony of Philoctetes in the turmoil of hatred and affection, would have been shared, in one form or another, by each member of the audience. Before the Athenian citizens assembled to watch this play, they had come through thirty years of warfare and political changes on which they had staked their life and fortune, whether they liked it or not. They saw that the war "waged by the Peloponnesians and the Athenians against one another" (Thuc., 1.1) to uphold the city of Athens, the school of Hellas (Thuc., 2.41), had turned out to be "a rough master who brings most men's minds down to the level of their actual circumstances" (Thuc., 3.82). They themselves had committed cruelties at the command of the generals. As the subject of the play is taken from the time when the siege of Troy has been forced to a dead end, so had Athens been driven to the last trench where the citizens could no longer talk of the war from the simple viewpoint of patriotism nor the leaders' policies as a matter of common weal. Had they been right in acting the way they had?

Philoctetes may thus be viewed, and most certainly was viewed by the Athenian audience in 409 B.C., as a rearranged account of the wartime problems, enlarged in a wider theme of universal human contact and interdependence through speeches where deceptiveness and ambiguity carried by words ensnares all the dramatic characters. They have to unravel the web of outward appearances to see reality before they make resolutions and decide their course of action. They have to choose between personal

102

sentiments and "sacred public cause." The audience find themselves also urged to consider and choose. If unquestioned precedence is to be given to the greater good of the greater number, as Odysseus maintains, if foreign policy is at the mercy of the egoistic competition of warmongers, as the Atreidae are described by Philoctetes, what is the right thing to do for each of the citizens placed in the same position in his relationship to his country as the characters of the play? Is victory of the whole army everybody's? Is one man's justice another's?

In the much-disputed scene of Heracles' epiphany,[36] Philoctetes returns to the Greeks and Odysseus' aim is fulfilled. This unexpected ending provides an attainment of the ultimate object of the drama and also a significant hint for our search for Sophocles' idea of tragic heroism. Therefore we may now recall the hero before ending our review of the play from the opposite angle. Philoctetes, who has shown as much resoluteness and fortitude in living up to chosen standards as that of any other Sophoclean hero, who has made it impossible even for his friend to break his will, now changes his mind. It is a total reversal of Philoctetes' earlier heroic decision.[37] However, it does not mean a surrender, nor a collapse, nor a defeat. It does not invalidate the hero's precious suffering and endurance. By refusing to help the Atreidae and Odysseus and facing starvation, he proved that he could still resent, as a free man, against the wickedness of the world, the injustice of the gods. His change of mind almost took place when his friend's appeal touched his heart (1350, 1352). He found it hard not to respond to the earnest and well-meant plea of a repentant noble youth. But he held his ground. He showed that he valued righteousness above everything else.

When Heracles, Philoctetes' spiritual father, elicits an obedient submission, Philoctetes' change of mind gives us a sense of blissful reconciliation, of a happy finale. What follows Philoctetes' voluntary change of mind is his rehabilitation and the victory of the whole Greek army. The audience have been feeling,

103

though convinced of and impressed by the heroic nobility of the man who fights with bare hands against the evil of human society, that going home to Malis with the diseased foot will not be the right thing for Philoctetes, that the hero ought to be cured and reintegrated. Philoctetes has indeed won. Soceity has lost the battle. Society has been made by this forsaken man to respect his rightness. Nevertheless, the play must not end even after the hero has proved himself invincible. In order to be reborn, to be regenerated to honor, society needs a hero. A hero, though logically incompatible with human society in which moderation and mutual cooperation are required of each member, is vital to its life. Only his heroism can resuscitate corrupt society. By returning to the Greeks and doing his part in the Greek army, Philoctetes ought to restore life and honor to himself as well as to his society.

The only thing that can give the hero an insight into this is his own divinity within himself. Philoctetes, like Ajax and other Sophoclean heroes, finishes his drama as a god reaching the realm of immortality through his hard-won victory.[38] But there is all the difference in the world between Ajax and Philoctetes. The immortality Ajax has won by refusing to change his mind, Philoctetes has acquired and consolidates through a pious change of heart.

The fact that the dramatist concluded the play in a healing tone of reconciliation and foregiveness, by a step taken by the hero himself, not by an arbitrator as in *Ajax,* is suggestive of the aged poet's idea of tragic heroism. In *Ajax,* the drama ends in tragic rupture. Although the disagreement on the dead hero's burial is settled by Odysseus' valuable "common sense," an abysmal chasm gapes at one's feet. On the contrary, one would sense in the comforting reconciliation of the last scene of *Philoctetes* the aged poet's optimistic vision of life that embraces both hero and society. One might also give thought to the end of *Oedipus Coloneus,* Sophocles' last play, where the hero whose family was under the gods' rage (965) is taken into the gods' arms through his death. The Sophoclean hero who has established tragic heroism by fighting against gods and human society is finally reconciled with both of them.

Old age may have brought these philanthropic sentiments to Sophocles' mind; one might also explain it with tolerance and leniency Sophocles must have acquired through the years of disappointments and regrets caused by the decline of the fortune of his home country. As Sophocles was no exception to being a creature of the age, one could perhaps discuss the matter in the perspective of socio-historical reality of the late fifth-century Athens, which I will try to do in chapter 5. But not irrelevant is the way the poet depicted Odysseus, the hero's opponent.

Sophocles did not make him a mere sample of despicable villainy.[39] We saw that the dramatist deliberately doubled the remoteness of the man who appeared as the ''agent''[40] of the army and the gods by veiling him in a mist of fake stories, thus illustrating the intricacies, both intellectual and moral, of the wartime problems in which each citizen is involved. But that dramatic aim can be achieved with fewer words in a simpler way, though perhaps less effectively. Why, then, has the poet spent time and words in such an intricate manner on this subordinate character? It is because, as it seems to me, the poet recognized in this unpleasant character appreciable qualities that need and deserve attention, if not vindication. Odysseus' self-effacing subservience to authority (as shown in Neoptolemus' ''story'') is to be valued in a militaristic regime. At the same time, there is something to be said for his strong longing for renown, his bent for gain and glory (as shown in the false merchant's ''story''). It can be ugly and offensive in itself, but it can also be a virtue that propels, say, warriors to martial achievements and to contribute to the cause of their community. Both of these qualities, strict self-control and desire for success and fame, are traditional Odyssean virtues. Could Sophocles leave the former unmentioned and the latter exposed to mere contempt and disdain?[41]

105

Sophocles is by no means asking the audience to approve of Odysseus' cause or method. His ability to improvise adjustments (980–83), another prominent quality of the relativist, was ineffectual. Yet in executing his "bluff," despite his brazenfaced statement before his disabled enemy, Odysseus refrains from the meanest violence.[42] His narrow escape from the danger (1293),[43] by which he manages to survive as he has always done, could have been ignominious, yet it is worth noting that the poet let this clever man of expediency manifest himself to be the target of Philoctetes' divine bow. His sanguineness and resilience when at the end of his tether may save him from possible attacks on the repulsive motivation of self-serving egoism. If Dio Chrysostom has found Odysseus of Sophocles "gentler and simpler than Odysseus of Euripides,"[44] what has enabled the poet to impose this impression upon an expert reader must be Sophocles' deep understanding and affection for this popular figure in literary tradition. The poet probably felt that this world of human beings poises itself on both Philoctetes and Odysseus. Playing an ungracious part for the greater good of the greater number, unpleasant as it is, could sometimes be of use to "deliver society from senseless destruction," while "passionate heroism, glorious as it is," could "disrupt society."[45]

By spending words and time and exploiting most elaborate dramatic technique on the hero's opponent, Sophocles prepared the way for reconciliation. For the society represented by Odysseus, although it has shown its many-sided selfishness, must live on. Odysseus' opportunist code sounded most detestable (1049)[46] when Philoctetes' intransigence appeared most admirable (1081–1217);[47] when Philoctetes showed himself most illogical but pious (1447), Odysseus' wider awareness of the world obtrudes itself.[48] In accordance to Zeus' will, the Greeks are to continue fighting on the Trojan battlefield. The hero's society must live on, reanimated and rehonored by his heroism.

Odysseus, in these preserved and lost plays, was, without doubt, each time a new creation. Sophocles must have made selective use of the versatile abilities and propensities given or hinted at in the Homeric archetype according to his dramatic purposes, while simultaneously developing the germ of other qualities. How, as a whole, did Sophocles value the Odyssean personality in his persuit of tragic heroism?

It was Sophocles who, taking over the heroic ideal of Homer, first established in tragic drama an idea of a hero rigorously respecting honor (*time*) as an absolute value, persisting stubbornly in defence of his principles against all advice and threats and dedicating himself to chosen standards even to the extreme of self-destruction. In spite of differences in personalities and circumstances, the Sophoclean heroes of the extant plays are all branded with this stamp of intransigence.[49] Odysseus, in whatever mixture of his archetypal characteristics he may appear in one or the other of his plays, must stand in polar opposition to these proudly lonely people of uncompromising virtue.

Sophocles' *Vita* (20) mentions his dependence on the *Odyssey* rather than on the *Iliad*: "He tells stories after the manner of the poet (Homer) and in many plays copies from the *Odyssey*." We have also seen, though incompletely, how frequently Sophocles has let Odysseus appear on his stage (see p. 89 and note 19). Why has Sophocles given him such ample opportunity for activity? Why has Sophocles spared so much skill for Odysseus in *Philoctetes,* as demonstrated in the previous section? The *Odyssey* lacks that brilliance and passion that one finds in the *Iliad*. Achilles, a prototype of the Greek aristocratic ideal, embodies resplendent but short-lived glory. On the contrary, Odysseus in the *Odyssey,* throughout the long journey home, survives adversities and afflictions by dint of his endurance, self-restraint,

107

resourcefulness, diplomatic skill in speech, and alert action. In perils, he does not hesitate to lie and to cheat his enemies. His cunning saves his life, and his tricks secure advantages for his people. One would agree that such qualities, although they are incompatible with Achillean nobility and can often be ugly and objectionable, are to be valued in the hazardous life of seafaring adventures. We do not know how much of the general assumption was in people's minds that Odysseus the landowner never volunteered to join the Trojan expedition; he was forced to become a warrior; he was compelled to engage in dangerous voyages. At any rate, his wisdom and resilience had been valued and loved by tradition. Sophocles is not the type of writer who allows his dislike and partialities to overcome his dramatic aims; his objective portrayal keeps his personal feelings hidden behind the fascinating creation of his dramatic poetry.

However, if in *Philoctetes* Odysseus' honor is preserved, if his strict self-repression in a corporate life is illuminated with "the ring of truth" of a skillful narration, if his insatiable aspiration for fame and undying desire for success are not condemned but rather protected from mere scorn by a distorting prism of a fake story set up between him and the audience, and if that changeability, dogged perseverance, and long-sighted historical vision in procuring the common good is made fruitful in the end, would not this indicate that the poet had a positive interest in these traditional virtues of Odysseus? Would not one feel in those exquisite devices of dramatic skill even an apologetic touch for his morally disputable characteristics?

It is often wondered how the *Iliad* and *Odyssey,* these two works of farily different nature, could have been produced by one poet. However, if we are persuaded that Homer did create both *Iliad* and *Odyssey* (of course with philological qualifications admitted), why in Sophocles' case is it not permissible to recognize, together with his ever-growing passion for and devotion to tragic heroism, sympathy, and forbearance for human weaknesses? If my brief survey over the two lost plays attempted in the preceding chapters adumbrated anything of the lost Sophocles, he could possibly have made a tragic hero of a man, for instance, who killed his own mother and became mad, not only of lofty champions of moralities. He could presumably compose tragic poetry out of a grotesque cannibal story in a barbarian country, not only out of high-toned debates in civilized society. Some other lost plays of Sophocles may have shown more of his sympathy, even love, for this traditional hero with many questionable moral qualities, but, nobody would object, with the virtue of *sophrosyne*.[50]

5.

Some Additional Remarks

When Aristophanes offered literary criticism of the three great tragedians in his *Ranae,* produced in 405 B.C., Sophocles was called εὔκολος (well-balanced, *Ranae* 82) and was given a special seat of respect. An image of a well-balanced man should rest primarily on his works as a poet. We may therefore be assured of the expertise as well as of the diversity of his dramatic production. But the word would not have been used for Sophocles, unless he had had a moderate involvement in the affairs of his contemporary society, unlike Euripides, who is said, perhaps in some malicious mockery but not without reason, to have held himself aloof from civil interests.[1] We may reasonably look back at the dramatist as an Athenian citizen who has lived through the glories and calamities of a great century and seek to understand his work in terms of his age.

But "topicality" in Sophocles is hard to discuss not simply because of difficulties in dating his plays.[2] It is fairly different from, *e.g.,* that of Euripides, whose direct expression of disapproval or protest, amplified by an emotional touch on the part of the writer, is easier to catch, even for the readers of the twentieth century. Sophocles seldom discusses current topics in an overt manner, but out of the drama of such harmonious clarity and intense power as the result of a successful distillation of the complexity and diversity of his experiences, he asks acute questions. The more unobtrusively they are put, the more universal is the significance they assume.

Topicality in Sophocles

To the eyes of contemporary spectators, the class contrast in the debating scenes of the last half of *Ajax* would have been salient. The antagonism between the Atreidae and the bereaved of the hero was not merely that between the powerful and the commanded. Teucer, a bowman, and the sailors represented those who in Athens in the middle of the fifth century B.C. were excluded from the citizenship that permitted its possessors to fight as hoplites.[3] They kept on gaining social status by their contribution in a series of marine engagements and the construction of the sacred edifices of the city.[4]

When Odysseus presented himself as a peacemaker capable of adjusting class tension and steering the community toward an honorable future, his god-sanctioned intellect and social virtue indicated by the word σώφρονας (*Ajax* 132) would have appealed as an appreciable quality in a new leadership of the new age of democracy.[5] On the other hand, the antisocial characteristics of Ajax would not have passed unnoticed. The more inspiring his claim is, the more negative his relationship to society becomes. The audience would have been impelled to query what would become of the aristocratic values that, personified in Achilles by Homer, had been passed down as a precious heritage of the ancient Greek sensibility and now were illustrated in a most exalted form in the suicide of Ajax, if the heroes were to be tamed in order to accommodate them in a *polis*-state. In any case, self-restraint and a cooperative attitude, as political virtues, had occupied the Greek mind over a long period of time, with a growing significance in life in the *polis*-state. In 458 B.C., Aeschylus enthusiastically applauded in *Oresteia* the repression of

111

individual ambition and cautioned against dissension and anarchism.[6]

Thirty years of regretted warfare greatly changes the semantic range of words, as well as the idea of social virtue. If the political climate of the immediate past, when *Philoctetes* was produced, is to be mentioned, fraud, treason, violence, and civil war, which followed the Sicilian failure, had made the Athenian citizens "approach each other with suspicion, as though every one had a hand in plots" (Thuc., 8.66). The revolution of the Four Hundred in 411 B.C., with which Sophocles as a *proboulos* was brought into direct contact,[7] and his disappointments in it must have impelled the poet to consider man's condition as part of the body politic.

When Neoptolemus in *Philoctetes* commented on Odysseus' concession, "You became sensible" (ἐσωφρόνησας 1259), how did the word sound to the ears of the Athenian citizens? In Neoptolemus' mind, "being sensible" is inextricably connected with his respect for the will of Philoctetes. To Odysseus, "being sensible" presupposes the victory and the welfare of the Greek army. But the problem does not seem to be as simple as that. Peisander, in 411 B.C., in order to persuade the Athenians to abolish democracy and adopt oligarchy for the sake of the "Common Welfare" (Thuc., 8.53 σωτηρία), used σώφρων as a party slogan.[8]

As I tried to illustrate in chapter 4, the wartime problems of patriotic feelings versus personal interests, of ethical principles versus practical demands, and so on are presented in *Philoctetes* first as an issue of human understanding or comprehension of reality. I dwelt on the experiences we have in our senses and minds when things turn out quite different from our reasonable and eager expectations; how we become uncertain of our understanding, which is based largely on communication in words.

That kind of sensation is most acutely felt when we are met with a rapid succession of changes, surprises, and unpredictable events, as in a national crisis. Note how well the sensation is depicted, for example, in the crisp description by Thucydides of the incidents of Athenian political history in 411 B.C. How many of the Athenian citizens would have expected, when Peisander, arriving from Samos, stepped forward to speak to propose oligarchy in the face of the violent opposition of the people, that things would so happen that he be appointed to make whatever arrangements seemed best to him with Alcibiades and Tissaphernes (8.53)? Who could perceive the fluctuation of the mind of an exile when Alcibiades, ostensibly speaking for Tissaphernes in the negotiation held at Magnesia, made extravagant demands? Had the Athenian representatives really been deceived all the time (8.56)?

The question of comprehension of reality through verbal communication is combined with the issue of moral decision in a peculiarly critical manner in the time of war and national emergency as in *Philoctetes*. If the parallel I find in *Philoctetes* with the contemporary Athenian mentality is valid to any extent, the bitter thoughts of the aged poet as a repentant *Proboulos*, who voted for what he assumed to be best in 411 B.C. (8.67), which turned out to be the worst (8.70–97), may be divined in the words and phrases of the characters of the play.[9] The whole action of *Philoctetes* is concerned with the hero's suffering and fight in the cause of the individual. Philoctetes' uprightness and defence of individual freedom were what was most needed when society grew so corrupt and individual conscience was put under control of party powers. The fact that the dramatist could afford the hero's change of mind only by dint of a *deus ex machina* would be suggestive of the difficulty in ethical problems of civil duty, but that he did provide it to bring victory to the Greeks attests to his unchanging love for his home country.

Whether *Epigoni* was relatively early or late, the play, with the moral question of matricide, would most certainly have appealed to the polemic spirit of the fifth-century Athenians. It is easily imaginable that divine injunction and paternal will had far more binding force in ancient times than they do for us moderns. "To honour gods, parents, and strangers" were the three great traditional commandments down to the end of the Athenian history.[10] Superiority of paternal relationships to maternal ones seems self-evident in *polis*-society that assembled citizens ran on definitely masculine principles.[11]

But, naturally enough in any history of human civilization and especially in one filled with commotion and confusion, the old sanctions and codes came to be doubted. These traditional relations between parent and child, between god and man, though deeply embedded in the structure of community to keep it solid and resilient, were to be reexamined and questioned sooner or later. The debate on filial duty in Aristophanes' *Nubes* (1409–1429) (dated 425 B.C.) and *Aves* (1346–1368) (dated 414 B.C.) may echo contemporary thoughts on the issue. One might also be reminded of how Jocasta scorns the authority of prophecy in *Oedipus Rex* (979).[12]

Since we cannot date the play, no substantial discussion can be attempted to inquire into how Sophocles' *Epigoni* bears on current topics. But its first production would have offered occasion for animated conversation with a question involving these issues: "Would this be justifiable homicide under the Draconian distinction?"[13]

Even if *Tereus* cannot be dated more specifically than "well before 414 B.C.," Sophocles' awareness of the social and political realities cannot be overlooked. The Thracians had become increasingly large in Athenian consciousness ever since the latter had caught glimpses of the former's life while engaging in the warfare along the northern route against the Persians. Before entering into alliance with Sitalces, then king of the Thracians, in the summer of 431 B.C., and making his son Sadocus a citizen, the Athenians had been wishing to benefit from the great power his father had possessed as the ruler of a territory covering more than half of Thrace (Thuc., 2.29).[14] They had hoped that Sitalces would overcome Perdiccas, who in conjunction with the Lacedaemonians threatened to encroach upon the Athenian power around Macedonia (Thuc., 1.57). To Athenian eyes, the Thracians were not to be cast aside as potential allies, yet they were "barbarians and beyond the pale."[15] Just as Tereus had helped Pandion,[16] so historical Thracian mercenaries were to play a prominent part in Athenian military affairs,[17] but they were also a cause of apprehension because of their uncouth and savage manner.[18]

If there was appropriateness in taking the bonds of wedlock between the Athenian and Thracian royal families in the play as analogous to the potential or actual political and military relationship between the two nations, the complete devastation as the result of the ill-fated marriage, with the last view of the country's reigning family gone (Fr.581R), must have appeared ominous to Athenian eyes. The whole misfortune, viewed on a human level, originated from the lustfulness of a Thracian king. Regardless of whether the poet intended or not, *Tereus* can be easily interpreted in terms of racial conflicts.

Topicality in Sophocles is indeed hard to deal with, but it is unmistakably there behind the captivating detail of his dramatic poetry and tells us about the doubts and regrets cherished by the poet and then fused into his mind and soul to make them broader and deeper.

If, by taking one of the fragments (Fr.589R) to recapitulate the whole action of *Tereus* and the metamorphosis to symbolize human diminution, I was not amiss in postulating a drama of human defeat, rather than of victory, as is usual in Sophoclean tragedy, the word used to sum up the heroine's and the Thracian's deed ἄνους, a typically Sophoclean word, would draw attention with its slightly different nuance: the story of an infatuated woman, wife of a barbarian king, invites us to consider the play, next, as one of the "un-Sophoclean" tragedies, yet as testimony to the poet's no small concern about the irrational in human nature.

115

Sophocles and the Irrational

As far as Fr.589R tells us, what occasioned such desolation was not so much tribal traits but the thoughtlessness of the sisters. The barbarian king is condemned as "lacking in reason—mad"; the Athenian princesses as "madder still." As Tereus gave his animal desire free reign, so Procne succumbed to brutality. She outdid Tereus in savagery. Eventually, all these mad people were alike metamorphosed into helpless beings. The Athenian women, though severely provoked, ought to have piously left the affair to Zeus (Fr.590R). Procne overstepped what was permitted to mortals.

This, however, may not be in the sense of Ajax—"not thinking as a man" (*Aj.* 761,777)—and other typically Sophoclean heroes. Sophoclean heroes, in the extant plays, are criticized as "lacking in reason," just as the same comment is made on the three principal characters of *Tereus:* Ajax is reproached for his foolishness (*Aj.* 763 ἄνους); Antigone is accused of being unwise (*Ant.* 99,562 ἄνους); Oedipus is rebuked for his folly (*OR* 626 οὐ φρονοῦντα). However, they develop their heroism out of their "foolish" choices: Ajax proves to be peerlessly magnificent through his suicide; Antigone triumphs over mediocrity; Oedipus, by promoting an obstinate quest for truth, shows an indomitable spirit. Their proud disdain of compromise, conventionalism, and hypocrisy drives them to destruction. But, notwithstanding the catastrophes in terms of ordinary human life, the heroes testify to the victory of humanity. In them, destruction and greatness are inseparably combined. In the light of their idealism, discretion, security, and modest standards of behavior are weaknesses. They incur ruin not through a lack of them but from their determined rejection of them. Their failure in terms of living the life of average people is a victory for human dignity. Their folly turns out to be the proof of their heroic temper. Their courage is proved by their ability to cross the boundaries set for mortals, even illogically.

What we are led to suppose, by an examination of Fr.589R and relevant facts, to happen to the characters of *Tereus* is very unlike what happens to the Sophoclean heroes in the extant plays. The sisters were also excessive in their behavior, but their excesses most probably ran not in the direction of self-elevation but of self-debasement. The metamorphosis into birds would indicate this. Procne's end cannot be called heroic. She is spared further disgrace. She is pitied and shown mercy to. She is kept yoked to an inhuman status. The criticism of her foolishness would not have been passed nor the comparison to a confused physician made if her deed had been a brave contempt and a deliberate disregard of human limitation. Excited by untrammelled anger and sexual jealousy, Procne debased herself, killing, cooking, and serving up her own son, in the same manner as Tereus debased himself by violating a virgin and cutting out her tongue.

This way of looking upon uncontrollable passion as the generator of harm and as being detrimental to human dignity would approximate to what we find in Euripides—notably, in *Hippolytus* and *Bacchae*. In both plays, emotional turbulence is regarded as an element that drives human existence to humiliation and annihilation, and reasonable control of these appetites is held as desirable to keep men and women decent and civilized. In Euripides' plays, the irrational in human nature working as a destructive power was personified in the divine figures of Aphrodite and Dionysus. The fragments of *Tereus* did not reveal much about divine intervention. Dionysus had to be searched on a precarious footing. But Aphrodite is also obvious, if the Greek way of thinking is to be followed. She would manifest herself to the Greek eyes in the most devastating aspect of her power, to drown mortals in sexual passion, deprive them of their worldly scruples, and drive them to destruction.

The irrational aspect of human nature viewed in such circumstances is not entirely lacking in Sophocles' extant drama. We have *Trachinae,* where sex is the leading theme.[19] I mentioned briefly the possible affinity and difference between *Trachiniae* and *Tereus* in connection with chronology. On closer examination, the two plays seem to have given a subtle contrast in their demonstration of the power of Aphrodite. When Deianeira, the wife of Heracles, discovers that the triumphant return of her long-missed husband has brought her the shame of "sharing a common couch" with another woman "wedded to one lord" (539), she applies a love-philtre—in fact, a poison given by a monster—in an attempt to retrieve her husband's love. The philtre causes Heracles' death, and Deianeira kills herself.

Deianeira's lament over her married life in the prologue is quite akin to Fr.583R, where Procne complains about the loneliness of her married life in a strange country. In both plays, a gentle lady suffers under the scorn of a wild or presupposedly wild husband. In *Trachinae,* Heracles is not a barbarian king; he is a familiar Greek hero. But his superhuman strength and monstrosity are the chief factors that cause the dramatic conflicts to take place. He saves Deianeira from Achelous, an inhuman being. But the raw element of the combat and the shadow of natural forces connected with his past labor persist in his present figure, and the destructive energy in his new activities outside home keeps him away from Deianeira's domestic existence.

The separation of Heracles and Deianeira is often pointed out by critics.[20] It is one of the dominating themes of the play. The two central characters never meet. The cleavage between them is intrinsic, because Deianeira's wish to retrieve absent married life works in a centripetal manner on principles of peace and safety, passivity and introspection, while Heracles' existence directs itself outward to deeds and activities. There is a qualitative contradiction between them: Deianeira, symbolizing civilized social life, is opposed to Heracles, who is made to represent the primitive beast-world. The gap is never filled in the play.

The peculiar impression of amalgamation that is inherent in the Procne legend and to which Sophocles seems to have given a deeper meaning cannot be neglected. The composite substances of the drama would have seemed to be heterogeneous in the early part of the play. The gap in the mismatched marriage would have seemed irreparable: the lonely wife wishing to make up for an unstaisfactory married life, her mental and emotional system tried to rediscover previous family ties and former surroundings (Frr.583R, 584R). Yet the Athenian princess, once given by her father to a barbarian king, is bound to him inseparably in the bonds of wedlock. In the course of the action, the man and wife with her sister and their son all become inseparable in a perverse manner. They are one. The father who begot the child consumes it to put into his own belly. The mother who gave life to her son destroys him. Is this contrast between basic conglutination in the Procne legend and dissociation in *Trachiniae* merely superficial, or does it have anything to do with Sophoclean idea of tragedy?

In *Trachiniae,* the destructive power of love spares neither the hero nor the heroine, but both preserve their dignity by committing suicide. Although both are helpless victims of that invincible goddess, Aphrodite, they still get the better of their respective deaths. Deianeira, in her pure devotion to Heracles, tries to die a faithful wife worthy of a true hero, as she has relentlessly tried to be all her life. When she finds that things turned out opposite to her intentions, she chooses death as the only possible way to atone for her error. She does not allow herself to be at the mercy of the workings of this unkind world, and thus to end by losing her identity. She does not throw herself prostrate to the indomitable force, to be pitied and metamorphosed into a bird. Exceptional among the heroines of the extant plays as she is, Deianeira is still "Sophoclean."

Heracles also dies a hero. His unpleasant self-centeredness and callous disregard of Deianeira's tender affection, which nevertheless produces his masculine greatness, is brought to perfection by his steely demand to his son to help him accomplish his suicide and to marry his concubine.[21] Heracles' undisturbed conviction that he is a hero guides him in his performance of his duties.

The deaths of these two central characters, each occupying

a separate half of the play's disjointed action, each summing up his or her life history in different forms of chosen deaths, give the *Trachiniae,* despite its various peculiarities among the extant Sophoclean plays, that outstandingly characteristic mark of Sophocles. Suicide, in Sophocles, can be a final stroke that ensures an individual to retain his or her integrity and honor.[22]

Procne's and Tereus' transfiguration, on the contrary, symbolizes their bruised life: the remains of their humanity disappear the moment they lose their human forms. If, like Deianeira, Procne had refrained from yielding to disgraceful passion, from indulging in revengeful desire, there would not have been such havoc. She could have ended a respectable Athenian princess. Her defeat could have been magnificent.

Sophocles' interest in the power of the irrational does not seem to be mere caprice, nor has *Trachiniae* been scooped up by accident to be one of the seven plays. He dramatized a story about a wife of Theseus, king of Athens, falling in love with her stepson in *Phaedra.* When Phaedra's love for Hippolytus is thwarted by the youth's rejection, she accuses him (of an attempted rape), reveals this to her husband, and then kills herself, as the legend tells us.[23]

Aphrodite would have been again prominent. Love is called an illness assaulting men and women with an overmastering power that even Zeus cannot evade (Frr.680R, 684R), which is precisely the same remark uttered by Deianeira (*Trachiniae* 443. *Cf. Ant.* 781ff). Whether Phaedra's foreign (Cretan) origin is stressed or not is not known, but it is assumable that she behaves as a respectable Athenian queen: in all probability it is Phaedra who twice calls love "a shameful thing" (Frr.680R, 679R). It seems that in Sophocles' version Theseus was believed to be dead (Fr.686R). Phaedra is, as it were, legally free to love Hippolytus.[24] Nevertheless, she seems to be very much ashamed of her passion for Hippolytus. It seems very likely that her strong sense of shame made Phaedra an afflicted woman forced to bear her passion as an invalid would endure a disease (Frr.680R, 684R).[25] How a woman who calls love "a shame" should come to let hers be known to the youth is hard to guess. It is conjectured that a letter is sent through a nurse.[26] In any case, she must get in touch with Hippolytus before she is rejected (Fr.678R?), as the story goes.

There is no evidence to prove that Sophocles made Phaedra commit suicide or that he followed the traditional legend in letting her falsely accuse the youth, but to a shame-conscious lady, defending her honor would have been her supreme concern. A self-imposed death to save her name could have made Phaedra another Deianeira.

At any rate, Phaedra, who gave her name to the play, must surely have won the sympathy of the audience as a central character should. If she is condemned to be a bad woman "having no reason" (Fr.682R), possbily by her husband after his incredible return alive,[27] Phaedra's inner struggle, failing to reach an unsympathetic mind, would suggest the same tragedy as that of Deianeira, who, proving to be Heracles' most obedient wife, is stigmatized by him as "treacherous" (*Trachiniae* 1050) for her seemingly malicious deed. As in *Trachiniae,* this complete absence of understanding of the agony of the heroine is cast into relief by the diptych form of dramatic structure (see p 118), so in the same way in *Phaedra,* the pitiful suffering of the heroine could possibly have been met with an insensitive lack of understanding in a disjointed second half of the action. For Phaedra, most probably carrying her drama to completion by letting her love be known to Hippolytus, that sequence must have formed one distinctive part to allow the return of Theseus to begin another.

It has been asserted that Sophocles' *Phaedra* is a criticism of Euripides' *First Hippolytus,*[28] in which the heroine herself made advances to Hippolytus. The young man, ashamed to face the woman, veiled his head.[29] The play was received unfavorably by the conventional Athenians.[30] Sophocles showed in his play how a woman should behave when overcome by such passion.[31] It is worth noting that Phaedra, in the *Second Hippolytus* of Euripides, clings to her ideal of honor (329ff, 403ff, 407ff, 488ff. *cf.* 498ff, 503ff) so anxiously that her speeches are filled with the notion of dying a virtuous woman:[32] on mere recognition of her "shameful love" (392ff) she is determined to die (275, as reported by the nurse). The idea of false accusation as revenge for the rejected love comes quite abruptly and is pronounced only once in the closing lines of her part (728–31). Euripides' emulation in making his heroine even more virtuous than Sophocles' Phaedra explains her preoccupation with guarding her honor. The *Second Hippolytus* was produced in 428 B.C.[33] Sophocles' *Phaedra* would most appropriately be dated not long before 428 B.C.

There may be some validity in supposing the three plays of Sophocles (*Trachiniae, Tereus,* and *Phaedra*), where the force of Aphrodite is or is very likely to be outstanding, to reflect or hint at the Euripidean influence (the borrowings and criticism being mutual) and in suspecting the typically Euripidean flavor, particularly in *Tereus*. The fact that the play was liked by the fourth-century audiences who favoured Euripides also hints at its possible Eudipidean flavor. The view suggested by the use of such significant words as ἀνουστέρως and θυμωθείς in a summing-up comment (Fr.589R) adumbrates the play as a drama on moral failure, a lack of regulation in the baser human appetites.

Little is known, from the studies of the extant plays, of Sophocles' concern about the power of the irrational in the sexual area of human nature, but a brief survey of these "un-Sophoclean" plays would indicate that he was not altogether hesitant to draw humanity in its frail bark of flesh tossed about by the storm of its own inner dark passion.

However, we notice in the condemnation of Procne for putting herself under the supremacy of the irrational (Fr.589R) a characteristic that makes Sophoclean drama so valuable in the history of human civilization. As in the extant plays, so in *Tereus*, the gods' irresistible force would have been overpowering: one can almost feel the presence of Aphrodite, Dionysus, and presumably others. But in spite of the absolute sway of the gods over this world, which the poet accepts with his renowned piety (*Vita* 12), Sophoclean drama is perfectly self-contained upon the human level. The token of a Sophoclean hero is his self-sufficiency. Dramatic characters complain that they have been subjected to the inscrutable power of the gods, and the Chorus repeatedly sing that everything in this world is ordained by Zeus (*Trach.* 1278, *Tereus* Fr.590R). But they are fully aware that human beings are responsible for the disaster, that people are to blame for the affliction they incur upon themselves. When Procne's own fault is explicitly pointed out, we are assured of Sophocles' conviction of self-determination.[34]

A belief in the free action of individuals presupposes and promotes a respect of individuality.[35] It may be rightly said that Aeschylus does not depict suffering of one individual but of a family and that there is no hero but an *oikos* in his drama.[36] If, on the other hand, Sophocles' surviving plays are marked with the estimation of individuality, their heroes, testifying to the value and dignity of individual human beings bear the honor of representing for us that memorable step forward in the history of human civilization. Their heroism reaches its heights as they fight against their gods and their people courageously and tenaciously in defence of individual human honor.

In the meantime, the question of the hero's reconciliation with the gods and human society would have occupied the poet's mind all his life, since he posed it in a most poignant manner in the scene of the discussion on Ajax's burial in *Ajax*. He is anxious to give solution in the last two extant plays. The supernatural element in the endings of *Philoctetes* (Heracles *ex machina*) and *Oedipus Coloneus* (the miraculous death of the hero as reported by the messenger) would indicate the fundamental difficulty of the problem. Nevertheless, the high morality the Sophoclean heroes chose to die for in adverse circumstances lived on and guided their own age and those that followed.

The view of the "selector," therefore, whoever he was, for whatever purpose he "selected," in whatever way he influenced the "selection," may have been fair enough and done justice to the essential quality of the Sophoclean drama. However, we would be well advised to bear in mind that the lost Sophocles is by no means negligible. What one would have called "un-Sophoclean" under the dazzling light of the poet's lofty idealism is by no means insignificant, as we glimpsed in his possible handling of the victim of an enjoined matricide or of an ill-fated marriage. As we saw in his handling of the villain's part in its relationship to the hero and his heroism in the next-to-last play, the aged poet's vision of life seems to have assumed greater dimensions than we presupposed. We saw him giving due consideration to the values contradictory to the hero's, to another individual, to pave the way for a reconciliatory ending of the play. Each one of us would be free to sense in that philanthropic touch the depth of his soul and the breadth of his mind, acquired along with the years of his work as a dramatic poet, or the tolerance and forbearance dearly bought through his experiences as an Athenian citizen. But if the tragic heroism of Sophocles, now reviewed in a wider context, should have greater appeal with its greater beauty and power, my discussion has not been idle.

Abbreviations

The book fragments of Sophocles are cited from S. Radt, *Tragicorum Graecorum Fragmenta*, vol. 4, *Sophocles* (Göttingen, 1977).

The fragments of Aeschylus are cited from H. J. Mette, *Die Fragmente der Tragödien des Aischylos* (Berlin, 1959).

Euripides fragments are quoted with the numbering of A. Nauck, *Tragicorum Graecorum Fragmenta*, second ed. (Leipzig, 1889).

When ancient works are cited, names and titles are abbreviated, as in the *Oxford Classical Dictionary*, second ed. (1970) or in comparable fashion.

Periodicals are abbreviated as:

AJP	*American Journal of Philology*
BICS	*Bulletin of the Institute of Classical Studies*
BSA	*British School at Athens, Annual*
CP	*Classical Philology*
CQ	*Classical Quarterly*
CR	*Classical Review*
CW	*Classical World* (successor to *Classical Weekly*)
GRBS	*Greek, Romand and Byzantine Studies*
Herm.	*Hermes*
HSCP	*Harvard Studies in Classical Philology*
ICS	*Illinois Classical Studies*

Mus. Helv.	*Museum Helveticum*
Philol.	*Philologus*
Phoen.	*Phoenix*
REG	*Revue des études grecques*
RevPhil	*Revue de philologie, de litterature et d'histoire anciennes*
Rh. Mus.	*Rheinisches Museum für Philologie*
RIL	*R. Istituto Lombardo di Scienze e Lettere, Rendiconti*
RivF	*Rivista di Filologia*
TAPA	*Transactions of the American Philological Association*
UCPCP	*University of California Publications in Classical Philology*
WS	*Wiener Studien*
YCS	*Yale Classical Studies*

Notes

1. Theomachy and the *Ajax*

1. Zeus in *Trachiniae* may be presented as the father of Heracles (*e.g.*, 1086), but in the closing lines of the Chorus (1278), his presence is felt to have faded into what might be called supreme power. Apollo in *Oedipus Rex,* giving a grim oracle to the young wanderer (788), which is later recalled bitterly by the blind king (1329), will perhaps be identified as a deity concerned with the fate of Oedipus, but he instantly diffuses into an impersonal force. The transition is swift and elusive.

2. The appearance of Athena, with its traditional formula of *hybris*-punishment, is criticized as an Aeschylean remnant not in harmony with the new Sophoclean view of tragedy by A. Lesky, *Die tragische Dichtung der Hellenen*[3] (Göttingen, 1972), 189–90 (henceforth, Lesky, *Tragische Dichtung*); and K. Reinhardt, *Sophokles*[3] (Frankfurt, 1947), 38 (henceforth, Reinhardt, *Sophokles*).

3. M. Haslam *apud* A.K. Bowman, ed. *The Oxyrhynchus Papyri,* vol. 44 (London, 1976), 1ff. (Radt number 10c)

4. Thamyras, who had great skill in lyre performance, being punished for his insolence of challenging the Muses, was a familiar figure in myth (*Il.* 2.594–600). In Sophocles' *Thamyras,* presumably a contest took place and then the Muses struck Thamyras blind. He was also deprived of his art of music (Fr.241R). That the blinding was represented onstage is evident from the fact that Thamyras' mask had one black and one grey eye (Pollux, *Onomasticon* 4.141). The actor showed the black-eye side toward the spectators after Thamyras was blinded (Schol. *Il.* 2.595. *cf.* Quintil., 11.3.74; A. Lesky, "Die Maske des Thamyris," *Anzeiger der Phil.-Hist. Klasse, österreichische Akademie der Wissenschaften* 8 (1951), 101ff; W. M. Calder III, "The Blinding, 'Oedipus Tyrannus,' 1271–74," *AJP* 80 (1959), 301 n.2. Contemporary vase-paintings, which were most likely to reflect scenes from Sophocles' play, if not

in precisely the manner in which he was seen in drama, show Thamyras' left side while hs is still in an unperturbed posture (before the blinding, Hydria of Vatican, *ARV²* (J. Beazley, *Attic Red-figure Vase-Painters²* [Oxford, 1963]), (1020. 92, Hydria of Naples 3143 *ARV²*, 1020. 93), his right side when in agony (after the blinding, Hydria of Oxford 530, *ARV*,² 1061, 152).

On the connection between vase-painting and drama and dating, see T.B.L. Webster, *Monuments Illustrating Tragedy and Satyr Play, BICS* Supp. 20 (1967), 152 (henceforth, Webster, *Monuments*) and *An Introduction to Sophocles²* (London, 1969), 200 (henceforth, Webster, *Introduction*); H. Froning, *Dithyrambos und Vasenmalerei in Athen* (Wurzburg, 1971), 75–77, 84–86; L. Séchan, *Étude sur la tragédie grecque dans ses rapports avec la ceramique²* (Paris, 1967, 1st edition, 1926), 193–98 (henceforth, Séchan).

5. As a contribution to R. Carden, *The Papyrus Fragments of Sophocles* (Berlin and New York, 1974), 171–235 (henceforth, Barrett, *Niobe*). (Radt number 441a)

*P. Oxy.*2805, first published by E. Lobel, *The Oxyrhynchus Papyri,* vol. 37 (London, 1971), 15–17 with Pl.V.

6. B.P. Grenfell and A.S. Hunt, *Greek Papyri,* series 2 (Oxford, 1897), no. 6(a); and B. P. Grenfell and A. S. Hunt, *The Hibeh Papyri,* part 1 (London, 1906), no. 11.

7. F. Blass, *Literarisches Zentralblatt* (1897), 334, and ''Vermischtes zu den griechischen Lyrikern und aus Papyri,'' *Rh. Mus.* 55 (1900), 96–101.

8. S. Radt, *Tragicorum Graecorum Fragmenta,* vol.4, *Sophocles* (Göttingen, 1977), 363–73.

9. C. Austin *ap.* Carden, *op. cit.*, 175 n.11ª; R. Kannicht *ap.* Radt, *op.cit.*, 364; W. Luppe, *Gnomon* 49 (1977), 329–30; W. M. Calder III, *AJP* 96 (1975), 411–12.

10. *Il.* 17.71, 24.525–33. *Od.* 4.181ff, 5.118ff, 8.565ff, (13.173ff), 23.210ff.

11. E. R. Dodds, *The Greeks and the Irrational* (Berkeley and Los Angeles, 1951), 29ff (henceforth, Dodds, *Irrational*).

12. Alcman, 1.16–18Page, Theognis, *Elegeia* 133–36, 141–42, 402, Semonides, 1.1ffBergk, Archilochus, frr.7. 7–9, 58, 74Diehl.

13. *E.g.,* Pindar, *Eighth Pythian* 61–80. Herodotus, 1.32, 7.46, 3.40, 7.10E.

14. Hesiod, *Erga* 9–29.

15. Solon 4.7. Diehl.

16. W. Schmid-O. Stählin, *Geschichte der griechischen Literatur* (Munich, 1934) 1.2 273 (henceforth, Schmid-Stählin).

17. See for pessimism of Sophocles in general, J. C. Opstelten, *Sophocles and Greek Pessimism* (Amsterdam, 1952).

18. See in general K. Reinhardt, *Aischylos als Regisseur und Theologe* (Bern, 1949); and O. Taplin, *The Stagecraft of Aeschylus* (Oxford, 1977) (henceforth, Taplin, *Stagecraft*).

19. Passing mentions are numerous. Succinct self-contained accounts are to be found in Schol. A. on *Il*. 24.602; Apollod., *Bibl*. 3.5.6.; Hygin., *Fab*. 9.2–4. For full bibliography, see A. Lesky, *RE* 17 I (1936), 644–706.

20. Schol. Eur. *Phoen*. 159; Lactant. on Stat., *Theb*. 6.117.

21. Whether Aeschylus wrote a trilogy is not inferrable from Artistotle, *Poetics*. 18.1456a.

22. H.J. Mette, *Die Fragmente der Tragödien des Aischylos* (Berlin, 1959), 95–101 (henceforth, Mette, *Fragmente*) and *Der verlorene Aischylos* (Berlin, 1963), 43–49 (henceforth, Mette, *Aischylos*). An excellent discussion on the scenes of Niobe's silence: O. Taplin, "Aeschylean Silence and Silences in Aeschylus," *HSCP* 76 (1972), 60ff (henceforth, Taplin, "Aeschylean Silences").

23. Fr.243aM = *Vita Aesch*. 6; Fr.273M, 6–7.

24. Fr.212M (= Ar., *Ran*. 911–24).

25. I follow Schadewaldt, "Die Niobe des Aischylos" in *Hellas und Hesperien* (Zurich and Stuttgart, 1960), 141–66, on the papyrus fragment first published by G. Vitelli–M. Norsa, *Bulletin de la société royale d'archeologie d' Alexandrie* 28 (1932), 107ff.

26. *Sept*. 769ff, *Ag*. 463ff, 792ff. More neutral use of *phthonos* in Sophocles, *El*. 1466, *Phil*. 776.

27. R. D. Dawe, "Some Reflections on *Ate* and *Hamartia*," *HSCP* 72 (1967), 89–123.

28. As F. Blass, C. Robert, "Archaeologische Nachlese," *Herm*. 36 (1901), 375; A.C. Pearson, *The Fragments of Sophocles* (Cambridge, 1917), (henceforth, Pearson) II. 100 and Barrett agree.

29. Sons of Niobe shot dead presumably while hunting on Cithaeron according to Schol. *Il*. A 24.602 and Apollod. or *in silva* according to Hygin., *Fab*. 9.3 (on Cithaeron?) or while exercising in *campus* according to Ovid, *Met*. 6.289ff. On the deaths of the boys reported by the *Paidagogos*, see W. M. Calder III, *AJP* 96 (1975), 412. As for the consecutive and separated deaths, first of boys, then of girls, by deities of their own sex, see Barrett, *Niobe*, 180 on *P. Oxy*. 2805 lines 9–10 and 228ff and Ovid, *Met*. 6.289ff.

30. Hdt., 2.53.

31. The anthropomorphism of the Homeric gods is plainly expounded in M. P. Nilsson, *History of Greek Religion* (Oxford, 1949), 134–79 (henceforth, Nilsson). *Cf.* H. J. Rose, *A Handbook of Greek Mythology*[4] (London, 1950), 109ff, 112ff, 134ff (henceforth, Rose).

32. Webster, *Introduction*, 200; G. Norwood, *Greek Tragedy*[4] (London,

1948), 173. *Cf.* on Thamyras in Nekyia of Polygnotus, see Paus., 10.30.8. F. Hauser, *Jahreshefte des österreichischen Archäologischen Institutes* 8 (1905), 35–41 connects it with the Oxford Hydria.

33. C. Robert, *Oidipus: Geschichte eines poetischen Stoffs im griechischen Altertum* II (Berlin, 1915), 92; U. von Wilamowitz-Möllendorff, *Griechische Verskunst* (Berlin, 1921), 347; and Webster, *Introduction*, 200.

34. An unabashed exhibition of Niobe's pride in her happiness, the actual deed of *hybris* of the heroine of the play, must precede the scenes of the children's death not merely to start the story but also as correlative to severe divine punishment in the Sophoclean design of theomachy. The supposed link between Ovid and Sophocles is too weak to allow a direct conclusion that the Roman poet imitated the play in his account of Niobe's misfortune and metamorphosis. But the uninhibited boasting in Ovid of Niobe on her large number of children, personal beauty, wealth, mighty royalty, and pride of ancestry, even to the extent of claiming for herself the people's worship given to Leto (*Met.* 6.165–203), may echo Sophocles. *Cf.* F. G. Welcker, "*Niobe* von Sophokles," *Zeitschrift für die Alterthumswissenschaft* 12 (1837), 105ff.

As for Ovid's derivation from Sophocles, a parallel consideration on the *Medea Hypothesis* is suggestive: C. Robert (*Bild und Lied*, Berlin, 1881, 231) ingeniously argues that the hypothesis to *Medea* was read by Ovid and that its information was used by him in *Met.* 7.159–296. See also O. Ribbeck, *Die Geschichte der römischen Dichtung* II (Stuttgart, 1900), 303. As to the possible connection of the accounts of Niobe of the mythographers to the *Niobe* hypothesis (of Sophocles), see Barrett, *Niobe*, 224.

35. G. Kinkel *Epicorum Graecorum Fragmenta* (Leipzig, 1877), 49 (henceforth, *E.G.F.*).

36. D. B. Monro, *Homer's Odyssey* I-XII[2] (Oxford, 1886), 104, 181, 220.

37. For bibliography on the rape of Cassandra, J. Davreux, *La Legende de la prophétesse Cassandre* (Bibl. Liège 94, 1942), 42ff.

38. "There is a play for each of those who fell in Troy. The plot against Palamedes, the anger of Nauplius, the madness of Ajax and the destruction of the other (Ajax) in the rocks."

39. Sophocles' preference for the representation of a court of law is pointed out by Schmid-Stählin, I.2. 316 n.1. On *OR*, B. M. W. Knox, *Oedipus at Thebes* (London and New Haven, 1957), 78–98, 114–89. For reconstruction of the play see: Th. Zielinski, "De Aiacis Locrensis Fabula Sophoclea," *Eos* 28 (1925), 37–49 (henceforth, Zielinski). He called *Ajax Locrus* a *tragoedia jurisjurandi*, as he called *Philoctetes tragoedia veritatis* and *Electra tragoedia ultionis*.

However, even the issue of chief importance is clouded with vagueness. "By force tearing away Cassandra" can be understood either as a rape or as mere physical violence. M. Oka ("Homer and the Epic Cycle," *Memoirs of the Faculty of Letters*, Kyoto University 16 [1976], 206) argues that in *Od.* 11.422 Agamemnon is said to have obtained Cassandra as his spoils of war, which is also related in *Iliu Persis*. Meanwhile in *Il.* 19.258–65 Agamemnon swears that he has not touched Briseis. If the same notion on sexual chastity is held in *Iliu Persis*, Agmemnon would not have accepted a Cassandra who had been raped. *Cf.* A. Severyns, *Le Cycle Épique dans l' École d' Aristarque* (Paris 1928), 363ff. The later tradition of accusation of a rape could have been derived from Odysseus' malicious slander, which is mentioned only in later accounts: Paus., 10.31.2; Apollod., *Epit.* 5.22; Callimachus, *Aetia* Fr.35 Pf.; Lycophron, 348ff; Quint. Smyrn., *Posthomerica* 13.422ff; Tryphiodorus, *Exidium* Il.2. 647ff; Eur., *Tro.* 1ff. Prosecution by Odysseus described in detail in Libanius, *Refutationes*, ed. Foerster 8 (Leipzig, 1915), 128ff.

40. Pearson, I. 10, also Zielinski, 39.

41. C. Robert, *Die Iliupersis des Polygnot* (Halle, 1893), 63. About the legend, Apollod., *Ep.* 6.20–22; see also G. Huxley, "Troy VIII and the Lokrian Maidens" in *Ancient Society and Institutions: Studies Presented to Victor Ehrenberg on his 75th Birthday*, ed. E. Badian (Blackwell, Oxford, 1966), 147–64.

42. *Supra* Lucianus, *De salt.* 46 (n.38).

43. Webster (*Introduction,* 202) recognizes a ring of grandiloquence in Frr.35R, 38R (both *Aechmalotides*). On identification of *Aechmalotides* with *Ajax Locrus,* see *infra* n.45.

44. Procl., *Chrest.* Schol.*Il.*1.37. 20f Dindf.; T.W. Allen, *Homeri Opera* V (Oxford, 1912), 22–23, 106.

On Ajax's suicide, W. B. Stanford, *Sophocles, Ajax* (London, 1963), XX (henceforth, Stanford, *Ajax*): "Homer does not explicitly state how, but probably he assumed that it was by suicide, as is generally accepted in the later tradition."

45. On chronology, for *Thamyras,* 468–461 B.C., see *supra* n.4. The testimonium for *Niobe* (before 422 B.C.) is Schol. to Ar. *Vesp.* 579. If *Antigone* 834 is a reference to his own play, it is before 442 B.C. (*infra* chapter 3, n.85). If Fr. Adesp. *Niobe* 7N² is from Sophocles' *Niobe* (attributed to Sophocles by Welcker, Dindorf, Valckenaer, Wilamowitz) the three word iambic may suggest early production (*cf.* W. B. Stanford, "Three Word Iambic Trimeters in Greek Tragedy," *CR* 54 [1940], 8–10). For *Ajax Locrus:* Zielinski (*art. cit.*) identifying the play with *Aechmalotides* proposed the "time before Polygnotus decorated the Stoa Poikile" in which the scene of Ajax's prosecution was painted (Paus., 1.15.2). His argument was accepted by Webster, *Introduction,* 202, 173.

The third actor recognized in *P. Oxy.*3151 Fr.4 8–13 does not exclude an

131

early date. Aeschylus in 458 B.C. used three actors. Athena's address to the Argives poses a difficult problem to Zielinski's proposition that the Chorus were the captive women, but not an unsolvable one, as Haslam admits. If *P. Oxy*.3151 Fr.9 2–4 can be brought into any connection with Fr.35R, and if Zielinski's identification and the dating are right, the play is early. Fr.41R will be a strong support. (On the date of the construction of Stoa Poikile, see L. H. Jeffery, "The Battle of *Oinoe* in the Stoa Poikile: A Problem in Greek Art and History," *BSA* 60 (1965), 41–51, who gives 462–1 B.C.) Sophocles' other plays with legendary *theomachoi*, such as *Laocoon, Tantalus,* and *Andromeda,* do not give us any hint that the theme of theomachy itself suggests early composition.

The preserved *Ajax* is generally assumed to be Sophocles' earliest extant play. Many critics, recognizing remarkable resemblances in form and content between *Ajax* and *Antigone,* are willing to place the production of *Ajax* not far from that of *Antigone.* I favor an earlier date. *Cf.* C.H. Whitman, *Sophocles: a Study of Heroic Humanism* (Cambridge, Mass., 1951), 42–43 (henceforth, Whitman, *Sophocles*); A. Lesky, *Geschichte der griechischen Literatur* (Bern, 1957/8), 257 (henceforth, Lesky, *Geschichte*). If the Ajax-lekythos, ascribed by Schefold and M. Robertson to the Alkimachos-maler (*ca.* 450) in fact illustrates Sophocles' Ajax, which I believe it to do, we have external evidence for dating: K. Schefold, "Sophokles' Aias auf einer Lekythos," *Antike Kunst* 19 (1976), 71–78. I owe this reference to Professor Calder.

46. An address to Thetis is to be recognized in the first play of Aeschylus' Ajax trilogy, *Armorum Judicium* (Fr.285M).

Cf. Schol. *Aj.* 762.

47. Athena with her attributes of martial characteristic, Rose, 107; A. Müller, *Lehrbuch der griechischen Bühnenalterthümer* (Freiburg, 1888), 236. On the appearance of Athena in the theater, critics have different ideas. Athena on ground: A. W. Pickard-Cambridge, *The Theatre of Dionysus in Athens* (Oxford, 1947), 48; Taplin, *Stagecraft,* 116 n.1; *cf.* Schol. *Aj.* 14. Athena on *theologeion:* W. M. Calder III, "The Entrance of Athena in *Ajax,*" *CP* 60 (1965), 114–16 and "Once More: The Entrance and Exit of Athena in *Ajax,*" *Classical Folia* 28 (1974), 59–61. Athena only as a voice: H. D. F. Kitto, *Greek Tragedy*[3] *(London, 1961), 151 (henceforth, Kitto, Greek Tragedy)* and Schmid-Stählin, I.2. 460, with whom I cannot agree.

48. B. M. W. Knox, "The *Ajax* of Sophocles," *HSCP* 65 (1961), 8 (henceforth, Knox, "*Ajax*"). Knox speaks of the "inferior" tone of the word. My point, in addition, is that an ally can turn into a rival at any moment.

49.R. P. Winnington-Ingram, *Sophocles, an Interpretation* (Cambridge, 1980), 14 (henceforth, Winnington-Ingram, *Sophocles*).

50. Echoed in 766, 770.

51. Knox, *"Ajax,"* 4.

52. Ajax, Antigone, Haemon, Eurydice, Deianeira, Jocasta, and Heracles, as we shall see in chapter 5.

53. Its importance was first recognized and interpreted as a soliloquy by F. G. Welcker, "Über den *Aias* des Sophokles," *Rh. Mus.* 3(1829), 43–92, 229–64. Knox has elaborated the "soliloquy" view: *"Ajax,"* 10ff. A recent review of interpretations of the speech is given by M. Sicherl, "The Tragic Issue in Sophocles' *Ajax,"* YCS 23 (1977), 67–98.

54. On the "heroic" meaning of καλῶς (honorably), see A. W. H. Adkins, *Merit and Responsibility* (Oxford, 1960), 158ff, 163ff (henceforth, Adkins).

55. Odysseus with his compassion (122) and generosity in persuading a reluctant Agamemnon to allow the burial of Ajax, appearing as the harbinger of the coming age of democracy after the departure of the period of aristocracy (represented by Ajax), has been pointed out by critics: Knox, *"Ajax,"* 24–26; N. O. Brown, "Pindar, Sophocles and the Thirty Years' Peace," *TAPA* 82 (1951), 20 (henceforth, Brown).

56. 756 τήνδ' ἔθ' ἡμέραν, μόνην, this reading of *P. Oxy.* 1615 adopted by Pearson rather than the medieval MSS τῇδε θἡμέρᾳ μόνῃ. "Only this day will Athena (continue to) vex Ajax." ". . . the death of Ajax will (then) be conceived in a much more direct way as a retaliation of the goddess": J. C. Kamerbeek, *The Plays of Sophocles: the Ajax* (Leiden, 1953), 158.

Calchas' words are ambiguous (their truth is twice queried, 746, 783). "Only today will the wrath of Athena vex him, no more" (756) sounds as if Athena's grace after today is meant, but the audience who noticed the ambiguity of Ajax's third speech sense that they can mean "he will die today." The Chorus too perceive their error at 784–86.

57. *Cf.* Winnington-Ingram, *Sophocles,* 40.

58. B. Snell, *Scenes from Greek Drama* (Berkeley, Los Angeles, and Cambridge, 1964), 69 n.27 (on Fr.361R) (henceforth, Snell, *Scenes*); and G. H. Gellie, *Sophocles, a Reading* (Melbourne, 1972), 250 (henceforth, Gellie).

2. Alcmaeon in the *Epigoni*

1. A former version of this chapter appeared in *GRBS* 18 (1977), 107–26. I owe thanks to Dr. J.R. Melville-Jones for his generous help in editing my English style.

2. Added by F. Jacoby from Eustathius, *Eustathii Commentarii ad Homeri Odysseam* Tomus I (Hildesheim and New York, 1970), 421.

3. Translation by Pearson, I. 134.

4. For the attribution of Fr.185R to Sophocles' *Epigoni,* F. G. Welcker,

Die griechische Tragödien mit Rücksicht auf den epischen Cyclus geordnet I (Bonn, 1839), 276 (henceforth, Welcker); O. Ribbeck, *Die römische Tragödie im Zeitalter der Republik* (Leipzig, 1875), 494 (henceforth, Ribbeck); L. Campbell, *Sophocles, Plays and Fragments* (Oxford, 1881), II. 502 (henceforth, Campbell); Pearson, I. 129; C. Robert *Die griechische Heldensage*[5] (Dublin and Zurich, 1967), III.1. 958 (henceforth, Robert, *Heldensage*).

5. For the attribution of Fr.186R to Sophocles' *Epigoni,* Welcker, 273; Ribbeck, 492; Robert, *Heldensage,* III.1. 958. A. Nauck, *Tragicorum Graecorum Fragmenta*[3] (newly edited by B. Snell, Berlin, 1964), 173 (henceforth, Nauck), putting it and Fr.185R among the Adespota, remarked, *"fortasse huius (Sophoclis) fabulae. . . ."* Pearson (I. 129) argues partly from Athen., 13.584d that the line quoted can be safely regarded as being from Sophocles, *Epigoni,* since it was one of his most famous plays and still popular in the fourth century B.C.

6. For the attribution of Fr.187R, in connection with Antiphanes, Fr.191 II90K, to Sophocles' *Epigoni,* Welcker, 278; Ribbeck, 495; Pearson, I. 69, 131, 133; Robert, *Heldensage,* III.1. 958.

7. For the attribution of Fr.201hR to Sophocles' *Epigoni,* Welcker, 276; Ribbeck, 494; Pearson, I. 138; Robert, *Heldensage,* III.1. 958.

8. E. H. Warmington, *Remains of Old Latin* (London: Loeb Classical Library, 1936), II. 420–29 (henceforth, Warmington). The text and English translation here given of Accius are all his, except for an occasional modernizing of a few words for clarity's sake and my revision of Frr.272–73 (taking *Illorum* as antecedent to *quos*) and of Frr.291–93, which I have translated according to the text as restored by Bergk and Ribbeck (*infra* n.10).

9. Welcker, 269; Ribbeck, 489; Robert, *Heldensage,* III.1. 958, and H. J. Mette, *Lustrum* 9 (1964), 116 (henceforth, Mette, *Lustrum*) regarded Accius' *Epigoni* as a translation of Sophocles' *Epigoni.* Pearson (I. 129) regarded it as being probably an adaptation, but did not feel certain about this.

10. Th. Bergk, *Rh. Mus.,* n.s.3 (1835), 84: *maneas adhis an te exilio macte pelopis externis* codd.: *ad Glisantem* Bergk, *exilio macte ex terris Pelopiis* Ribbeck.[3]

11. For the identification, Welcker, 269ff; Ribbeck, 489ff; Pearson, I. 132; Robert, *Heldensage,* III.1. 958; Bethc, *RE* I (1894), 1552 *s.v.* Alkmaion, VI (1909), 462 *s.v.* Eriphyle (henceforth, Bethe); Webster, *Introduction,* 174.

Against identification: Nauck and Campbell and Radt printed separately; W. N. Bates, *Sophocles, Poet and Dramatist*[2] (New York 1969), 197. Not separation but not identification: Schmid-Stählin, I.2. 437.

12. As sons of Amphiaraus, only Alcmaeon and Amphilochus are recorded by mythographers; *cf. Od.* 15.248. As daughters, Eurydice and Alcmena are

134

mentioned once by Pausanias (5.17.7) and Demonassa three times (3.15.8, 5.17.7, 9.5.5).

13. So Welcker, 273; Ribbeck, 491; Robert, *Heldensage*, III.1. 958; Mette, *Lustrum*, 117.

14. Cicero's own translation (?), or possibly he cites Accius, while Cleanthes would have used Sophocles.

15. Ribbeck (492) saw fraternal confrontation in Fr.186R, but he found in Amphilochus a son eager to save his mother. Welcker (273) interpreted it as spoken by Alcmaeon on his discovery of Eirphyle's second bribery. Robert, *Heldensage*, III.1. 958, assigned it to Alcmaeon.

16. For detailed discussion, see Mette, *Lustrum*, 76, and H. D. Jocelyn, *The Tragedies of Ennius* (Cambridge, 1967), 236 (henceforth, Jocelyn).

17. Jocelyn (30) gives as one of the data the percentage of trimeters in Latin measurable verses compared with that of Greek tragedy.

18. Warmington Frr.87, 88–89, 93–94. So Ribbeck, 483; F. Leo, *De tragoedia romana* (Göttingen, 1910), 10; Mette, *Lustrum*, 113.

19. As to whether Eirphyle was killed within the dramatic time in both plays, see *infra* the discussion on Eriphyle and Alcmaeon.

20. For the interpretation of this fragment, see *infra* n.48.

21. Welcker, 270ff.

22. *(N)Jbb* Supp. 17 (1890), 180ff (cited by Pearson, I.137).

23. Jacob supposed (*Nachtr. zu Sulzer*, IV 123, cited by Welcker, 269, and Pearson, I. 132) that *Eriphyle* dealt with the earlier expedition of the Seven. Is he sound? The strongest argument for nonidentification is that Accius' *Epigoni* as well as *Eirphyla* (only once) are cited. But the substitution for the true title of the name of one of the principal characters was not infrequent. Ribbeck (493) regarded them as the same play. Pearson left the matter an enigma (I. 132 n.1).

24. "Matricide before expedition" is supported by Welcker (270), Ribbeck (489), and Robert (*Heldensage*, III.1. 958). Schmid-Stählin (I.2. 438) and Pearson (I. 130–31) have left it unsettled, since they are not happy with the slow attack of the Furies after the expedition. Bethe (*Thebanische Heldenlieder*, Leipzig, 1891, 129ff; *RE* I, 1552) thought that there were previously two versions, *Thebais* (matricide after expedition) and *Alcmaeonis* (matricide before expedition), but did not say which version Sophocles' *Epigoni* followed. The ending of the play, as here conjectured, would settle the problem.

25. The text and English translation by J. G. Frazer, *Apollodorus* I[4] (London: Loeb Classical Library, 1961), 379ff.

26. So Welcker, 272; Pearson, I. 130; Robert, *Heldensage*, III.1. 957.

27. So Ribbeck, 493; Pearson, I. 131 n.1; Robert, *Heldensage*, III.1. 958.

28. So Ribbeck, 493.

29. Warmington (427) recognizes Harmonia's robes in Fr.289W. The earliest reference to Harmonia's robe is Hellanicus, *FGrHist* 4 F98.

30. Ribbeck (492) assigned to his ghost Frr.*Inc. Inc. Trag.* Accius(?), 25–26, 27–28.

31. The text and English translation by C. H. Oldfather, *Diodorus Siculus* III[3] (London: Loeb Classical Library, 1961), 27ff.

32. *Supra* n.6.

33. Astydamas (Arist., *Poet.* 14.1453b), Agathon, Euaretos, Nicomachus, as given by Bethe I, 1552.

34. *Infra* nn.64 and 66.

35. So Welcker, 270; Mette, *Lustrum,* 117. A plural title should be taken to give the identity of the Chorus. It is, however, not altogether unreasonable to suppose that women, say, waiting women of the palace, formed the Chorus (*infra* n.38), while the title referred to those whose fortune was the subject of the play as in Aeschylus' *Septem. Cf.* A. E. Haigh, *The Tragic Drama of the Greeks* (Oxford, 1896), 397.

36. *Ant.* 155–62, 376–83, 526–30, 626–30, 801–805.

37. So Ribbeck, 489; Robert, *Heldensage,* III.1. 948; Mette, *Lustrum,* 116.

38. I owe this suggestion to the referee of my paper in *GRBS* 18 (1977).

39. Schmid-Stählin, I.2. 116 n.2.

40. *Infra* n.71.

41. On the prologue of *Inachus,* see W. M. Calder III, "The Dramaturgy of Sophocles' *Inachus,*" *GR(B)S* 1 (1958), 143.

42. Thersander as the speaker of Frr.272–73W, Welcker 274. Of Frr.272–73W, 275W, and 274W, Ribbeck, 489; Warmington, 421.

43. So Ribbeck, 490.

44. So Ribbeck, 490. If Frr.277–79W indicates the disappearance of the Epigoni, they must reenter before the *agon* of the brothers (second episode, as supposed here) to sing the first stasimon. An exit of the Chorus within the action of the play is difficult in itself, *e.g.,* Eur., *Hel.* 386–514, *Alc.* 747–860, *Rhes.* 565–673. These difficulties and the theme of family conflict might urge one to consider another possibility (*cf. supra* n.35) for the Chorus.

45. So Ribbeck, 490.

46. Ribbeck (493) and Mette (*Lustrum,* 117) severed Fr.286W from Fr.280W and assigned the former to Eriphyle, ordering Demonassa to reveal the danger mentioned in Frr.284–85W, while Welcker (273) assigned it to Alcmaeon and noticed a sequence in Frr.277-79W—280W—286W, but not on the oracle, as I propose.

47. *Supra* n.13.

48. Welcker (273) and Ribbeck (491) did not hesitate to assign Fr.201fR to the same speaker as Fr.281W and did not see the tone of Fr.201fR as expounded in this chapter. I follow the punctuation of Nauck, interpreting: "How am I, being mortal, to struggle against the heaven-sent destiny, as hope of escaping it does not help the matter at all, when her death is destined."

49. Ribbeck (491) and Warmington (425) regard the words as being uttered by her son eager to save Eriphyle but assume Amphilochus as the speaker.

50. Sophocles often introduces a new character at the beginning of the third episode: the messenger from Teucer in *Ajax*, Haemon in *Antigone*, the Corinthian messenger in *Oedipus Rex*. As to a four-epeisodia structure, see *infra* chapter 3, n.58.

51. So Ribbeck, 494. Welcker, with much reason, combines it with Fr.942R. Text of Fr.201dR, μόναι codd. μόνης Radt.

52. So Welcker, 275.

53. Eriphyle's appearance with the intention of allaying the gods' rage is suggested on the strength of Acc., Fr.290W and on the analogy of Jocasta in *OR* 911ff and Clytaemnestra in *El.* 630ff by Robert, *Heldensage,* III1.1 958 and Mette, *Lustrum,* 117. But see note 67 on Fr.290W, and if she is in the least repentant of her first treachery, she cannot easily be bribed, nor would she try a second persuasion on her son.

54. Skillful use of stage properties and deft visualization of ironic situation is characteristic of Sophoclean tragedy, as pointed out by H. D. F. Kitto on Orestes' urn (*Sophocles, Dramatist and Philosopher,* London, 1958, 32ff); on Philoctetes' bow by P. W. Harsh, "The Role of the Bow in the *Philoctetes* of Sophocles," *AJP* 81 (1960), 408ff (henceforth, Harsh); and by G. M. Kirkwood on Ajax's corpse (*A Study of Sophoclean Drama,* New York, 1958, 95). See in general for props in tragedy: J. Dingel, "Requisit und szenisches Bild in der griechischen Tragödie" *apud* W. Jens, *Die Bauformen der Tragödie* (Munich, 1971), 347–67 (henceforth, Jens, *Bauformen*).

55. So Ribbeck, 494. Fr.189R, if these were the words of Alcmaeon accursing Eirphyle, must have been uttered after the temporary exit of Eirphyle urged by Demonassa to escape the danger. For Eriphyle must be absent from the scene where Demonassa reveals the second bribery to Alcmaeon.

56. For the catastrophe placed in the fourth episode in early plays of Sophocles, see K. Aichele, "Das Epeisodion" *apud* Jens, *Bauformen,* 71.

57. So Ribbeck, 493. Neither can Fr.287W be spoken by Amphilochus, nor can Fr.288W, Fr.185R, or Fr.289W be addressed to Amphilochus, if the assumption on Amphilochus' attitude to matricide proposed in this chapter be reasonable.

58. So Ribbeck, 488 n.1. This is from Accius, *Eriphyla.*

59. So Ribbeck, 494.

60. So Welcker, 276; Ribbeck, 494; Robert, *Heldensage*, III.1. 958 and *supra* n.4.

61. So Ribbeck, 494 and *supra* n.29.

62. *Proverb. Append.* 3.35.

63. Ribbeck, 494. Also Welcker (276) and Robert (*Heldensage*, III.1. 958) failed to see the horrified Eirphyle in Fr.201hR, which Pearson (I. 139) noticed.

64. Pearson (I. 131) regards it as highly probable. Robert (*Heldensage*, III.1. 959) gives, as a similar example of a relative appearing to take vengeance Eur., *Or.* 356ff.

65. For elucidation of this fragment, see Ribbeck 495; Pearson I. 136: προσῆκον Gaisford: προσηκόντως A, προσόντως M, προσόντος *vulgo*. εὐθυμίαν? Dindorf: εὐρυθμίαν F. W. Schmidt: εὐφημίαν *codd*.

66. *Philol.* 48 (1889), 554ff.

67. So Ribbeck, 495; Pearson, I. 131.

68. Eur., *Or.* 1ff, *HF* 1005ff.

69. ἄπελθ'· ἐκείνης *codd.:corr.* Nauck. ἰητρὸν *codd*.

70. *Supra* n.24.

71. Cic., *Div.* 1.40.80 and Paus., 1.34.3.

72. Paus., 9.8.6, 9.9.4; *Supra* n.10.

73. κατοικήσοντ' Blaydes: κατοικήσαντ' L, Radt.

74. W. Schadewaldt, *Monolog und Selbstgespräch* (Berlin, 1926), 93ff. Also 51, where he finds its root in Aesch., *Prom.* 88ff. *Cf.* E. Fraenkel, "Zwei Aias-Szenen hinter der Bühne," *Mus. Helv.* 24 (1967), 82ff, where Fraenkel sees "meditation" characteristic in Eteocles' speech (*Sept.* 653–76).

75. B. M. W. Knox, "Second Thoughts in Greek Tragedy," *GRBS* 7 (1966), 225 (henceforth, Knox, "Second Thoughts").

76. W. M. Calder III, "Sophocles' Political Tragedy, *Antigone*," *GRBS* 9 (1968), 389 (henceforth, Calder, "*Antigone*"); and D. L. Page as introduced in J. M. Bremer, *Hamartia: Tragic Error in the Poetics and in Greek Tragedy* (Amsterdam, 1969), 139 n.1.

77. *Antigone* 1096 εἰκαθεῖν, 1099 πείσομαι, 1102 παρεικαθεῖν, 1105 ἐξίσταμαι. B.M.W. Knox, *The Heroic Temper: Studies in Sophoclean Tragedy* (Berkeley and London, 1964), 67–75 (henceforth, Knox, *Heroic Temper*); "Second Thoughts," 216.

78. H. Patzer, *Hauptperson und tragischer Held im Sophokles' Antigone* (Wiesbaden, 1978) offers a reviewing discussion on the subject, concluding that Antigone is the central character (103).

79. W. M. Calder III, "A Reconstruction of Sophocles' *Polyxena*," *GRBS* 7 (1966), 56 (henceforth, Calder, "*Polyxena*").

80. Calder, *"Polyxena,"* 47; O. F. Gruppe, *Ariadne* (Berlin, 1834), 595.

81. E. Rohde, *Psyche* (English translation by W. B. Hills, London, 1925), 320 (henceforth, Rohde).

82. Aeschylus, *Xantriai* Fr.169N² = 368M (frenzy to madden the Bacchae) may be added.

83. But *cf.* A. W. Gomme, "The Position of Women in Athens in the Fifth and Fourth Centuries B.C." in *Essays in Greek History and Literature* (Blackwell, 1937), 89–115; H. D. F. Kitto, *The Greeks²* (Chicago, 1964), 219–36 (henceforth, Kitto, *Greeks*).

84. Winnington-Ingram, *Sophocles,* 205ff (chapter on "Furies in Sophocles"); and Dietrich, 91–156.

85. Anapaestic systems employed in *Antigone* must be regarded as an echo of the ancient manner. Among extant Greek tragedies an anapaestic *parodus* is found only in Aeschylus' *Prometheus Vinctus, Persae, Supplices,* and *Agamemnon,* Sophocles' *Ajax,* and *Inachus,* and Euripides' *Alcestis.*

86. It seems that Accius in *Antigona* (Mette, *Lustrum,* 113) and Ennius in *Iphigenia Aulidensis* (O. Skutch, *Rh. Mus.,* 96 [1953], 193–201), for example, used choruses different from those of their models. On how the Roman poets treated choruses, see Jocelyn, 30ff.

3. Sophocles and the Non-Greek World: *Tereus*

1. An earlier version of this chapter was read at a Greek-Latin drama discussion meeting held at Edinburgh University on June 3, 1981. I am grateful to Professor D. M. MacDowell of Glasgow University and to Professor E. K. Borthwick of Edinburgh University for their kind invitation. I benefited much from the discussion that followed.

2. W. Kranz, *Stasimon* (Berlin, 1933), 108 (henceforth, Kranz); P. Friedländer, "Die griechische Tragödie und das Tragische Dritter Teil," *Die Antike* 2 (1926), 104; *cf.* K. Reinhardt, *Vermächtnis der Antike* (Göttingen, 1960), 352.

3. Suidas *s. Sophocles. Cf. Vita* 18.

4. U. von Wilamowitz-Möllendorff, *Analecta Euripidea* (Berlin, 1875, reprinted by Hildesheim, 1963), 137–43 (henceforth, Wilamowitz, *Analecta*).

5. C. H. Roberts, "Literature and Society in the Papyri," *Mus. Helv.* 10 (1953), 270; W. S. Barrett, *Euripides, Hippolytus* (Oxford, 1964), 51–53 (henceforth, Barrett, *Hippolytus*).

6. Aeschylus wrote seventy plays, Euripides ninety-two, according to Suidas.

7. But on the source of *Vita* and a sceptical view of the "lives" of the

139

Greek writers, see M. R. Lefkowitz, "The Poet as Hero: Fifth-Century Autobiography and Subsequent Biographical Fiction," *CQ* n.s.28 (1978), 459–69 and, more fully, *The Lives of the Greek Poets* (Duckworth, 1981).

8. Phyrnichus was fined on account of his presentation of the *Fall of Miletus* (Hdt., 6.21). According to *Vita* 8–9, Aeschylus left for Gela when the Athenian audience preferred Sophocles. Euripides left for Macedonia (*Vit.* 124). On the assumption that Euripides was possibly put to heresy trial (Satyrus, *Vit. Eur.* fr.39 col.x), see W. M. Calder III *CP* 55 (1960), 128 and Lesky, *Geschichte*, 411. Agathon left for Macedonia (Ar., *Ran.* 83–85). Aristophanes was accused by Cleon (Ar., *Ach.* 377–82).

9. Phyrnichus, Fr.31K; Ar., *Ran.* 78, 82; *Vit.* 22.

10. *Vit.* 10; Thuc., 1.116; Plut., *Per.* 8. *Cf. infra* n.11 on *Strategos*. Surely he attended the games at Olympia or Delphi, although we do not have it attested.

11. As *Hellenotamias* 443 B.C. (*IG*, I² 202, 1.36); as *Strategos* (three generalships? *Vit.* 1, Ion *ap.* Athenaeum, 13.603e, Thuc., 1.116, and Plut., *Per.* 8 as *supra* n.10, Suidas *s.* Melissus (441–40 B.C.) and the second one *Vit.* 9. The last one Plut., *Nic.* 15 and Ar., *Pax* 695, but it is asserted that there was only one generalship, *i.e.*, that of 441/440 B.C., by L. Woodbury, "Sophocles Among the Generals," *Phoen.* 24 (1970), 209ff); as *Proboulos* after the Sicilian failure, 413 B.C. (Arist., *Rhet.* 3.18.1419a; for bibliography and discussion of the evidence, see *GRBS* 12 (1971), 172–74 with ns.114, 115). On doubts about Sophocles' political services except the generalship in 441/440 B.C., see H. V. Avery, "Sophocles' Political Career," *Historia* 22 (1973), 509ff.

12. It is true that cases for the reflection of Greek tragic performance on vase-paintings are dubious (A. W. Pickard-Cambridge, *The Dramatic Festivals of Athens* (Oxford, 1953), 176; W. M. Calder III, *G(R)BS* 1 (1958), 138), but this one for Sophocles' *Andromeda* by Webster is strong: Webster, *Monuments*, 147 and *Introduction*, 203. *Cf.* K. M. Phillips, Jr., "Perseus and Andromeda," *AJA* 72 (1968), 1ff; E. Simon, *Das antike Theater* (Heildelberg, 1972), 33. Webster dated the play soon after 460 B.C. Fr.135R may be a word referring to a Persian garment.

13. F. Jacoby, *RE* Suppl. 2. *s.* Herodotus, 237.

14. Plut., *an seni* 785B.

15. J. Rasch, *Sophocles quid debeat Herodoto in rebus ad fabulas exornandas adhibitis* (Leipzig, 1913).

16. The journeys of Herodotus ranged over the three continents known at that time. He traveled as far as the northern coast of the Black Sea (4.16–17); he went down the Nile to Elephantine (2.29); to Babylon in the East (1.181, 185) and Kyrene in Libya in the West (2.181).

17. His liberalism and Ionian sense of the world is suggested by H. Diller, "Die Hellenen-Barbaren Antithese im Zeitalter der Perserkriege" in *Grecs et Barbares, Fondation Hardt Entretiens sur l'antiquité classique* VIII (1961), 65 (henceforth, *Fondation Hardt*).

18. Plut., *De Herod. Malignitate* 857A.

19. H. Schwabl, "Das Bild der fremden Welt bei den frühen Griechen" in *Fondation Hardt*, VIII 3–23 and I. Weiler, "Greek and Non-Greek World in the Archaic Period," *GRBS* 9 (1968), 21–29.

20. Although there is a pointed contrast of two forces moving to war at the beginning of the *Iliad* 3. (*cf.* 4. 429–36).

21. B. Snell, *Die Entdeckung des Geistes*[3] (Hamburg, 1955), 151 (henceforth, Snell, *Entdeckung*).

22. I owe much of my discussion on Aeschylus and Euripides in this aspect to suggestions made by Professor E. K. Borthwick and to H. C. Baldry, *The Unity of Mankind in Greek Thought* (Cambridge, 1965), 36ff; and H. H. Bacon, *Barbarians in Greek Tragedy* (New Haven, 1961), 132ff (henceforth, Bacon).

23. Coincidence between *Andr.* 215–18 with Hdt., 5.16 is mentioned by W. Nestle, "Untersuchungen über die Philosophischen Quellen des Euripides," *Philol.* Supp. 8 (1901), 652–54. Other coinciding ideas pointed out by J. Wells, *Studies in Herodotus* (Oxford, 1923), 187: *Hel.* from Hdt., 2.112–20, *IT* from Hdt., 4–103, criticism of tyranny *Supp.* 447–55 from Hdt., 5.92 and others. Kranz (109–12) observes Euripides' preoccupation with the problem of Greek-barbarian antithesis: natural rule of the Greeks over barbarians *Andr.* 647–54, 662–67, *IA* 952–54, 1264–75, 1400–1401, the superiority of the Greek rule of law to the barbarian concept of tyranny, *Med.* 591–92, 1330–1343, *Andr.* 173–76, 243, 261–62, 870, *Hec.* 328–31, 877, 1129, *Or.* 485, 1110–1115, 1508, 1527, *Bacch.* 481–83, *IA* 270–72.

24. Bacon, 160 n.35.

25. U. von Wilamowitz-Möllendorff, *Einleitung in die Attische Tragödie* (Berlin, 1889), 31–32 with n.57. Wilamowitz also makes the point (4–5) that in general for Aeschylus the enemies are barbarians; for Euripides, other Greeks.

26. Bacon, 86.

27. Sophocles' dramatization attested by Tzetzes on Hes., *Op.* 566, which also shows the close adherence to his version by the later mythographers. References before Sophocles: Hom., *Od.* 19.518, Hes., Fr.125Rz, *Op.* 568, Sappho (in Hephaes.), Fr.88, Aes., *Ag.* 1146, *Supp.* 60–67; *cf.* Ar., *Av.* 280, Eur. Fr.773N,[2] *Rhes.* 545 (Soph., *El.* 107, 148).

28. So G. Mihailov, "La legend de Téreé," *Annuaire de l'Universitè de Sofia* Faculté des Lettre 50/2 (1955), 93 (henceforth, Mihailov); Robert, *Heldensage*, II.1. 156.

29. P. Parsons, ed., *The Oxyrhychus Papyri*, vol. 42 (London, 1974), 46ff, *P. Oxy*.3013. On the possibility that the mythographical accounts on Niobe (Apollod., *Bibl*. 3.5.6, Schol. *Il*. A 24.602) could also be traced back to the hypothesis of Sophocles' *Niobe*, see Barrett, *Niobe*, 224.

30. Wilamowitz, *Analecta*, 184; *cf*. R. Pfeiffer, *History of Classical Scholarship* (Oxford, 1968), 195.

31. C. Gallavotti, *RivF* 61 (1933), 177ff.

32. Now collected by C. Austin, *Nova Fragmenta Euripidea* (Berlin, 1968) (henceforth, Austin, *Nova Fragmenta Euripidea*) and M. W. Haslam, "The Authenticity of Euripides, *Phoenissae* 1–2 and Sophocles, *Electra* 1," *GRBS* 16 (1975), 150 n.3 (henceforth, Haslam).

33. The papyrus is attributed to the second or third century A.D. On the probable process of transmission, see T. Gelzer, "Sophokles' *Tereus*, eine Inhaltsangabe auf Papyrus," *Jahresbericht 1976 der Schweizerischen Geisteswissenschaftlichen Gesellschaft*, 183ff (henceforth, Gelzer).

Parsons points out as similarities with the Euripidean summaries the initial proper name, verbs in the past tense, and ambitious vocabulary.

34. Haslam (152) resumed Gallavotti's suggestion and argued partly on the ground of the data that G. Zuntz, in *The Political Plays of Euripides* (Manchester, 1955), 129ff, used in denial of Dicaearchus' authorship.

35. Sext. Emp., *Math*. 3.3.

36. Apollod., *Bibl*. 3.14.8; Schol. Ar. *Av*. 212; Conon, 31; Liban, *Narrat*. 4.1103; Achil. Tat., 5.5; Eustath., *Od*. 1875; Nonnus, *Dion*. 4.321, 12.75; Tzetzes, *Chilliad*. 7. 459ff.

37. So Ribbeck, 577; Warmington, 543; Mette, *Lustrum*, 124ff.

38. Jocelyn, 236. *Cf. supra* chapter 2, n.17.

39. T. B. L. Webster, "Classical Background to Racine's *Phèdre*," *Modern Miscellany presented to Eugene Vinaver* (1969), 304 (henceforth, Webster, "Classical Background to Racine's *Phèdre*").

40. Welcker, 374ff; W. M. Calder III, "Sophocles, *Tereus*: A Thracian Tragedy," *Thracia* 2 (1974), 87ff (henceforth, Calder, "*Tereus*"); Ribbeck, 579ff.

Gelzer (191) offers a different reconstruction. *Cf. infra* n.90.

41. Translation by R. Crawley, *The History of the Peloponnesian War* (London: Everyman's Library, 1910), 89.

42. Daulis is supported by Conon, 31; Zenobius, *Cent*. 3.14; Nonnus, *Dion*. 4.321; Paus., 10.4.9; Strabo, 9.3.13.

43. So W. Buchwald, *Studien zur Chronologie der attischen Tragödie* (Königsberg, 1939), 34 (henceforth, Buchwald).

44. So Calder, "*Tereus*," 87.

45. Calder, *"Tereus,"* 88.

46. On children in Greek tragedy, see G. M. Sifakis, "Children in Greek Tragedy," *BICS* 26 (1979), 67–80.

47. Calder, *"Tereus,"* 88.

48. Also Schmid-Stählin, I.2. 460. Thracian kings themselves claimed descent from Hermes (Hdt., 5.7).

49. Apollod., *Bibl.* 3.14.8.

50. *Cf. supra* chapter 2, n.39.

51. 10 ἀγήθη (sic) Scaliger, ἀληθῆ SMA, ἀήθη B (Paris, 1985) teste Gaisford, probaverunt Blomfield, Campbell, Buchwald. ἀγηθῆ v. Horworden.

52. So Welcker, 380. The text and Egnlish translation of Accius given here are all by E. H. Warmington, *Remains of Old Latin* (London: Loeb Classical Library 1936), II 542–49.

53. So Welcker, 377 and Ribbeck, 579.

54. For a different interpretation, see Mette, *Lustrum,* 125.

55. So Calder, *"Tereus,"* 89; Warmington, 542.

56. So Buchwald, 40 and Robert, *Heldensage,* II.1. 157; Ribbeck to the Chorus (580). Pearson (225) and Welcker (381) interpret it as the words of consolation directed to Procne after she has learned about the outrage. Outrage by Tereus cannot be "what is sent by the gods," which can only mean an unexpected death.

57. So Calder, *"Tereus,"* 89.

58. This would be an exception to the common "unity of time." Lapses of time should not be supposed in the reconstruction of lost plays as a rule. The reversal of one's fortune in one single day was the point of Sophoclean tragedy (*e.g., Aj.* 131). Gelzer settled the question by conjecturing that the incidents before the day of the feast were somehow narrated in the course of the action, the woven cloth arriving on the same day. This would require three-epeisodia structure instead of four, as usual in Sophocles (Jens, *Bauformen,* 50–51) and as presented here. But my epeisodia arrangement is, of course, tentative. *Cf.* on Euripides' *Stheneboea,* D.L. Page, *Greek Literary Papyri*[2] (London: Loeb Classical Library, 1942), 127, where two long intervals are supposed during the action of the play.

59. *Cf.* Apollod. and Achil. Tat. =*peplos,* Nonnus =*chiton.* F. Studniczka, "Beiträge zur Geschichte der altgriechischen Tracht," *Abhandlungen archäologischepigraphischen Seminares der Universität Wien* 6.1 (1886), 134 demonstrates that *peplos* and *chiton* in the three dramatists are interchangeable words of indefinite meaning. The robe Deianeira sends to Heracles is sometimes *peplos* (602, 674), sometimes *chiton* (580, 612, 769).

60. So Welcker, 380. Other examples of indefinite expression, masculine,

referring to both sexes: *Ant.* 455; Eur., *Med.* 1018.

61. Pearson, II.221 and also Ribbeck, 580 on the strength of Achil. Tat., 5.3.5.

62. Ribbeck, 580, "des Sophokles würdig."

63. So Welcker, 381.

64. Nurse speaks to Procne if a three-actor scene is presented, but it is not inferrable from either Fr.587R or Fr.647W.

65. On Maenads' attire, see Rhode 257. Dodds, *Irrational* 278 has shown that Euripides' description of the Bacchants in *Bacchae* is not a mere product of imagination, but reflects much of an actual cult.

66. Pearson, II. 231.

67. Calder, *"Tereus,"* 89.

68. The text and English translation by F.J. Miller, *Ovid, Metamorphoses* I² (London: Loeb Classical Library, 1960), 331.

69. Calder, *"Tereus,"* 90. *Cf.* Taplin, "Aeschylean Silences," 94 with n.113.

70. Buchwald, 36; I follow Welcker, 383. Mihailov (111) places it at the end of the drama, where, he supposes, Tereus prays to the sun to reveal the crime of the Attic women and help him in his retribution on them. As for the sun surveying the world, *cf. OC* 869.

71. σέβας Bothe: σέλας A.

72. ".... like a Tereus, a Thracian mercenary, shaking his dart and his target to boot."

73. Webster, *Monuments,* 152 gives: a fragment of Caivano Painter Dresden PV 2891 (330/310 B.C.); a fragment of Skyphos, Painter of Berlin Dancing Girl (430/420 B.C.) with inscription; a loutrophoros, late circle of Dareios Painter Naples 3233; M. Schmidt has seen in the picture by Dolan Painter on a bell-krater in Louvre (CA 2193 dated 400–370/60) a scene from Sophocles' *Tereus:* the cloth into which Philomela has woven her misery is being presented to Procne. The presence of the king does not necessarily mean that he was onstage during that scene. In addition, E. Simon, *Festschrift des Kronberg-Gymnasiums* (Aschaffenburg, 1968), 155ff. Apollodorus writes that Tereus pursued the women with a double-edged axe (*pelekys*), Scholiast to Ar., *Av.* 212 a sword (*xiphos*), Ovid *ferrum.*

74. Scholars are insistent that Tereus and the sisters were not represented on stage after the metamorphosis, but merely reported. But Professor E. K. Borthwick has made an interesting suggestion that the audience would see the appropriateness of the hoopoe metamorphosis if on stage Tereus was costumed in the Thracian manner of hair-style *(akrokomoi)* and headgear and that a birdlike Tereus presupposed in Aristophanes' *Aves* would be acceptable in a conven-

tionalized mask (cf. D. W. Thompson, *A Glossary of Greek Birds* (London, 1936), the frontis piece).

75. E. Oder (*Rh. Mus.*, 43 [1888], 54ff) and others (Ribbeck, Pearson, Robert, Buchwald, Mihailov, Calder, Radt) supported Welcker's proposition. U. von Wilamowitz-Möllendorff (*Aischylos Interpretationen* [Berlin, 1914], 28 an.3) doubted; Nauck printed among Aesch. Adesp.

76. As for the ascription not to the Chorus (Welcker, 383, which seems impossible) nor to the messenger (Jebb and Pearson, II. 231) but to the divine character, see Buchwald, 40, Calder, *"Tereus,"* 90, and Schmid-Stählin, I.2. 479 n.5.

77. Buchwald, 42.

78. Translation by C. M. Bowra, *Sophoclean Tragedy* (Oxford, 1944), 61; H. F. Johansen, *General Reflections in Tragic Rhesis* (Copenhagen, 1959), 168 counts it among the few anapaestic closings of Sophocles.

79. Dactylo-epitrite, *OR* 1086, *Aj.* 172.

80. Translation by Headlam (Pearson, II. 238).

81. So Buchwald, 34.

82. Calder, *"Tereus,"* 91; Kitto, *Greeks,* 202. *Cf.* U. von Wilamowitz-Möllendorff, *Kleine Schriften* (Berlin, 1935), I.17ff. For a full study of the Euripidean handling of the Medean legend, W. H. Friedrich, "Medeas Rache" *apud* E. R. Schwinge, ed., *Euripides* (Darmstadt, 1968), 177–239.

83. Consequently dated before 431 B.C. *(Medea* after *Tereus),* Buchwald, 35; Webster, *Introduction,* 4, 176; Calder, *"Tereus,"* 91.

84. *Hercules Furens* as dated between 414–413 B.C., mainly on metrical considerations, by T. B. L. Webster, *The Tragedies of Euripides* (London, 1967), 163 (henceforth, Webster, *Euripides*).

85. Calder, *"Tereus,"* 91 and M. Pohlenz, *Die griechische Tragödie* I² (Göttingen, 1954), 229. Pohlenz recognizes Euripidean influence from *Trachiniae* onwards. Webster (*Introduction,* 4) has noted in *Trachiniae* correspondences with Euripidean plays, which fall between 438–417 B.C. The most recent discussion of dating of *Trachiniae* is in Winnington-Ingram, *Sophocles,* 341–42. An analysis of the lyric meters of H. A. Pohlsander, *AJP* 84 (1963), 280 puts it between *Antigone* and *Oedipus Rex,* but nearer *OR,* accepted by D.S. Raven, *AJP* 86 (1965), 225. *Cf.* T. C. W. Stinton, *CQ* n.s. 27 (1977), 67–72. For early dating, see also E. R. Schwinge, *Die Stellung der Trachinierinnen im Werk des Sophokles* (Göttingen, 1962); S.G. Kapsomenos, *Sophokles' Trachinierinnen und ihr Vorbild* (Athens, 1963).

Antigone is usually dated to 442 B.C. *Cf.* U. von Wilamowitz-Möllendorff, *Aristoteles und Athen* II (Berlin, 1893), 298. For the dating of *Oedipus Rex,* see B. M. W. Knox, "The Date of the *Oedipus Tyrannus* of Sophocles," *AJP*

77 (1956), 133–47, who dates to 425 B.C. (henceforth, Knox, *"Oedipus"*). *Cf.*
W. M. Calder III, *Gnomon* 48 (1976), 601–604.

86. Dated between 431–425 B.C. by L. Gernet on historical considerations,
Mélanges offerts à O. Navarre (Toulouse, 1935), 207; not long after 429 B.C.
by I. Cazzaniga, *La saga di Itis nella traditione letteraria e mitografica gre-coromana* I (Milano, 1950), 45 and after him Mihailov; between 428–425 B.C.
by R. Goosens, *Euripide et Athènes, Mém. Acad. Roy. de Belgique* Classe des
Lettres (Brussels, 1962), 298 n.18 (henceforth, Goosens).

87. *BSA* supp. 3 (1966), 89–92.

88. M. Robertson, *A History of Greek Art* (Cambridge, 1975), 286–87;
P. N. Boulter, *AJA* 84 (1980), 385–86; J. Carter, "Procne and Sophocles,"
AJA 85 (1981), 189.

89. Besides *Tereus,* Schmid-Stählin, I.2. 479 n.5 give *Syndeipnoi*
(Fr.562R), *Tyro* (Pearson, II. 273). It is essential to the role of Heracles in
Philoctetes that he was recently a man.

90. Gelzer (191) postulates Procne as a self-respecting, genuinely "So-phoclean" heroine, while he pictures Tereus as a rude barbarian. But Procne
is condemned to be no less thoughtless than Tereus (Fr.589R, *anous-anousteros,*
no differentiation in the use of language).

91. Iphigenia in *Iphigenia in Tauris* is illiterate. If the famous passage in
which the illiterate herdsman described the letters that make up Thesues' name
in Euripides' *Theseus* was contemporary, the scene would be all the more
effective. *Theseus* is dated by Webster (*Euripides,* 101) before 428 B.C.

92. *Cf.* Ov., *Met.* 6.459–60: "His own passionate nature pricked him on,
and, besides, the men of his clime are quick to love: his own fire and his
nation's burnt in him."

93. *Cf.* E. R. Dodds, *Euripides, Bacchae* (Oxford, 1953), 402–16 (hence-forth, Dodds, *Bacchae*).

94. Winnington-Ingram, *Sophocles,* 91–116. *Cf.* C. Segal, "Sophocles'
Praise of Man and the Conflicts of the *Antigone,*" *Arion* 3 (1964), 2.58.

95. Rohde, 256.

96. There is none among Sophocles' lost plays that is indisputably known
to have treated a Dionysiac theme as the subject. *Tympanistae* could be sus-pected. It perhaps dealt with Phineus' sons and their step-mother (E. Herkenrath,
Berliner Philologische Wochenschrift 50 (1930), 332, Pearson, II. 311 ff). But
which god was worshipped by the tympanon-bearers is not known (Winnington-Ingram, *Sophocles,* 109). Dodds (*Bacchae,* xxvi) gives *Hydrophoroi* as a pos-sible case. On the possibility of Sophocles' *Bacchae,* depending on the con-troversial reading of the "Danaid papyrus" (*P. Oxy.* 2256 fr.3), see A. F.
Garvie, *Aeschylus' Supplices, Play and Triolgy* (Cambridge, 1969), 9. He
thinks it "not impossible" to attribute Frr.862R, 959R and also Frr.846R, 773R

to Sophocles' *Bacchae*. For *Athamas, cf.* Pearson, I. 3. *Dionysiskos* (satyr play) may also be noted.

97. R. P. Winnington-Ingram, *Euripides and Dionysus* (Cambridge, 1948), 156–57.

98. In *Ajax*, the third episode begins with the messenger from Teucer; in *Antigone* with the appearance of Haemon; in *Trachiniae* with the sudden anxiety of Deianeira; in *Oedipus Rex* with the arrival of the Corinthian messenger; in *Electra* with Orestes' appearance before Electra.

99. Barbarian Medea view: D. L. Page, *Euripides, Medea* (Oxford, 1938), xix; Schmid-Stählin, III. 360; L. Meridier, *Euripide* I (Paris, 1926), 118. Opposite view: B. M. W. Knox, "*Medea* of Euripides," *YCS* 25 (1977), 218ff (henceforth, Knox, "*Medea*"); V. Benedetto, *Euripide, teatro e società* (Torino, 1971), 33.

100. M. P. Cunningham, "Medea APO MECHANES," *CP* 49 (1954), 152.

101. Knox, "*Medea*," 220.

102. H. C. Baldry, "The Idea of the Unity of Mankind," *Fondation Hardt*, VIII. 175.

103. Pearson, II. 233, translation by Headlam; O. Reverdin, "Crise spirituelle et Evasion," *Fondation Hardt*, VIII. 89; Dodds, *Irrational*, 76 and 94 n.80 describing Dionysus as "not aristocratic god," open even to slaves.

104. Gelzer, 188. For the vases suggesting its popularity, *supra* n.73.

4. Sophocles and Odysseus

1. Probably more frequently than Aeschylus (who had Odysseus appear in *Psychagogoi, Penelope, Ostologoi, Circe* [Satyr drama], *Judgement of Arms, Philoctetes,* and *Palamedes*) and Euripides, in *Hecuba, Rhesus* (if Euripidean), *Cyclops* (Satyr drama), *Philoctetes, Palamedes.*

2. *Vita Soph.* 4. *Cf. Vita Aesch.* 15.

3. Notably in books 2,3,9, and 19. *Cf.*, Xenophon, *Mem.* 4.6.15.

4. *E.g., Nemean* 8.25–34.

5. *Nausicaa* (Odysseus' appearance not attested but cogently proposed by Pearson, II. 92–94; dated not long after 468 B.C. by Séchan, 167; Webster, *Monuments,* 149, and *Introduction,* 200).

6. It has been noticed that Athena's last words (132) sound rather like the closing comments of a tragedy than those of a prologue; Stanford, *Ajax,* on 127; Pohlenz, 173; I. M. Linforth, "Three Scenes in Sophocles' *Ajax,*" *UCPCP* 15 (1954), 5.

7. *E.G.F.,* 18; Pearson, II. 115–18.

147

8. *E.G.F.*, 19.

9. In Euripides' *Iphigenia in Tauris*, Iphigenia bitterly refers to Odysseus' deceit (24, 542), which is most likely to be an echo of Sophocles' play, as Th. Zielinski, *Tragodumenon* (Krakau, 1925), 271–72 affirms. *Cf.* W. H. Friedrich, "Zur *Aulischen Iphigenie*," *Herm.* 70 (1935), 96–100.

10. R. Pfeiffer, "Die *Skyrioi* des Sophokles," *Philol.* 88 (1933), 1–15; Carden, *op. cit.* (chapter 1, n.5), 94–109; Séchan, 185–92.

11. Robert, *Heldensage*, III.2. 1133 n.2; E. Wüst, *s.v.* Odysseus *RE* XVII, 1929–1931; F. Stössl, "Die Palamedes-Tragödien der drei grossen Tragiker," *WS* 79 (1966), 93–101 (henceforth, Stössl).

12. Stössl, 96.

13. φλοίσβου μετὰ κόπον in the sense of "after buffeting the waves," see Pearson, II. 134.

14. Both in Aeschylus' and Euripides' *Palamedes*, Palamedes is seen speaking as the defendant in the first person singular. The fragment from Euripides (Fr.578N²) shows him enumerating his general contributions to civilization, namely writing and its various uses (overseas letters, wills, contracts), which profited "human beings (*tois anthropois*)." Aeschylus' Palamedes draws attention to his service in wartime, but not specifically to the provision of military discipline (Fr. 304M: "I arranged for an army to have triarchs and leaders of a hundred. And I put meal-times in order, breakfast, lunch and supper as the third.") The speaker of Sophocles' Fr.479R, arguing for the defendant in third person singular, looks back on the role Palamedes played in a time of hardship, which all the fellow Greeks shared and managed to come through. There is a strong emotional appeal to the deep feelings, common to the comrades who experienced the same sorrows and joys in the labors of the voyage and the war.

It is unlikely that Nauplius, father of Palamedes, as suggested by Pearson (II.134), is the speaker. There is no story that tells us about Nauplius' arrival or stay in Troy during the Trojan War, except that he came to exact retribution for the death of his son in Aeschylus' *Palamedes* (Fr.305M), which Apollodorus (*Epit.* 6.8) epitomized and Schol. Eur. *Or*, 432 mentioned. All other stories about his revenge imply that he stayed at home. The speaker of Fr.479R knows about the famine and speaks as if he himself shared all these hardships in the expedition. Can Nauplius speak, even if he came to Troy hurriedly, in such a sympathetic tone? To me, Odysseus seems to be the only possible speaker.

15. *Rhet.* 3.15.1416b.

16. The settlement of Teucer in Cyprus was traditional: Pind., *Nem.* 4.46ff; Aesch., *Pers.* 897; (Eur., *Hel.* 148).

17. P. Venini, "Sui Niptra di Pacuvio," *RIL* 87 (1954), 175–87, proposed

that they are separate plays that Pacuvius combined. On Sophocles' dependence on the *Odyssey*, see p. 107.

18. Note how close this is to the story of the death of Heracles at the end of *Trachiniae* (1157ff). Heracles "learns too late" what a death by a resident in *Hades* means. Sophocles' successful employment of the "late-learning" motif in the middle plays, *i.e.*, *Trachiniae* and *Oedipus Rex*, is noteworthy. *Cf.* Hdt., 3.64, where Cambyses dies in Ecbatana and "learns the truth too late."

19. C. R. Post, "The Dramatic Art of Sophocles as Revealed by the Fragments of the Lost Plays," *HSCP* 33 (1922), 6.

Nothing can be ascertained about the *Euryalus*, which Eustathius cites only briefly (*Od*. 1796.52). Other titles in possible connection with Odysseus: *Ajax Locrus* (chapter 1, n.39), = *Aechmalotides* (?), *Antenoridai* (Pearson, I. 86–90), *Request for Helen* (Pearson, I. 121–26; Séchan, 181–84), *Polyxene* (?) (Calder, *"Polyxena,"* 38).

20. D. Seale, "The Element of Surprise in Sophocles' *Philoctetes,"* *BICS* (1972), 94–102; P. E. Easterling, *"Philoctetes* and Modern Criticism," *ICS* 3 (1978), 28–39 (henceforth, Easterling, "Modern Criticism"); Winnington-Ingram, *Sophocles*, 281; *cf.*, H. C. Avery, "Heracles, Philoctetes, Neoptolemus," *Herm*. 93 (1965), especially ambiguity about the "father" of Philoctetes, 290ff (henceforth, Avery).

21. Readers may be reminded, as the topics of recent controversy, *e.g.*, lines 839–42, so far interpreted almost unanimously as "oracular" hexameters to illuminate Neoptolemus' insight into the meaning of the gods' words (*e.g.*, Whitman, *Sophocles*, 183; Easterling "Modern Criticism," 34; J. S. Kieffer, "Philoctetes and *Arete,"* *CPhil* 37 (1942), 48 (henceforth, Kieffer)), reinterpreted by Professor Winnington-Ingram to be "heroic" hexameters indicating that the "prize" (841) is not the bow but Philoctetes: Winnington-Ingram, *Sophocles*, 283 and *BICS* 16 (1969), 48–50.

Lines 1054–1062, whether Odysseus is bluffing, now that he has control of the bow that provided Philoctetes with the necessities of life and promised his future glory, or he has really changed his mind and decided that the bow is enough. "Bluff view": Reinhardt, *Sophokles*, 196; A. J. A. Waldock, *Sophocles the Dramatist* (Cambridge, 1951), 213; I. M. Linforth, *"Philoctetes,* The Play and the Man," *UCPCP* 15 (1956), 136 (henceforth, Linforth); H. D. F. Kitto, *Form and Meaning in Drama* (London, 1956), 98, 124; Gellie, 152. "Serious view": D. B. Robinson, "Topics in Sophocles' *Philoctetes,"* *CQ* n.s.19 (1969), 45 (henceforth, Robinson); Tycho von Wilamowitz-Möllendorff, *Die dramatische Technik des Spohokles* (Berlin, 1917), 304–307 (henceforth, Tycho); Lesky, *Tragische Dichtung*, 244; O. Taplin, "Significant Action in

Sophocles' *Philoctetes,''* *GRBS* 12 (1971), 35, 44 (henceforth, Taplin).

Lines 1222–1260, that here is a play within a play by which Neoptolemus, pretending to have repented his shameless deed, tries afresh to secure Philoctetes, proposed by W. M. Calder III, "Sophoclean *Apologia:Philoctetes,''* *GRBS* 12 (1971), 153–74 (henceforth, Calder, *"Apologia''*); Taplin (28) also remarks that the return of the bow may have been part of the strategy (1232).

22. On 1402 εἰ δοκεῖ, στείχωμεν, : Tycho, 311. On the Scholiast's remark that Neoptolemus is deceiving, Calder, *"Apologia,''* 167; A. J. Podlecki, "Power of the Word in Sophocles' *Philoctetes,''* *GRBS* 7 (1966), 243 n.20 (henceforth, Podlecki).

23. A significant echo from the repetition of the word in the early part of Neoptolemus' renewed overture 1268, 1269, 1272, 1278, as pointed out by P. E. Easterling, "Repetition in Sophocles," *Herm.* 101 (1973), 29.

On the general function of the word *logos* and other words, see Podlecki, 233–50, especially 245, on the important difference between *logoi* and *mythoi* in the last scene of Heracles' epiphany. Also, A. E. Hinds, "The Prophecy of Helenus in Sophocles' *Philoctetes,''* *CQ* n.s. 17 (1967), 67–80 (henceforth, Hinds).

24. R. Takebe, *"Antilabae* in Greek Tragedy," *Journal of Classical Studies* 16 (1968), 42, classifying *antilabae* according to their function, explained that they are *"Antilabae* completing scenes.''

25. On the trochaic ending of a play bringing a logical but unacceptable conclusion in *Helena* (412 B.C.) and its technical influence upon *Philoctetes* (409 B.C.), see T. Drew-Bear, "The Trochaic Tetrameter in Greek Tragedy," *AJP* 89 (1968), 395 and 399. Also M. Imhof, "Tetrameter-szenen in der Tragödie," *Mus. Helv.* 13 (1956), 131.

26. Easterling, "Modern Criticism," 29.

27. Calder, *"Apologia,''* proposed an interpretation of Neoptolemus' story as "one whole lie," arguing from parallel uses of the present perfect form of *pleo* (sail), the number of the ship and crew, and the tradition about Thersites that Neoptolemus has not been to Troy. I have been completely convinced by him. In *Ilias Parva (E.G.F.,* 36–37), Neoptolemus' departure was narrated as an independent story after Philoctetes' return to Troy. It was most probably Sophocles' innovation to change the order of the events and make Neoptolemus Odysseus' partner in this play.

28. The contrast of the epithet of *Odysseus dios* in 344 and Philoctetes' epic periphrasis *Odysseos bia* in 314 echoed by Neoptolemus in 321 and by the merchant in 592 has been pointed out by A. F. Garvie, "Deceit, Violence and Persuasion in the *Philoctetes,''* *Studi classici in onore di Quintino Cataudella* 1 (Catania, 1972), 218 (henceforth, Garvie).

29. The false merchant scene is convincingly elucidated as a preparation for the transition from deceit to force (to be followed by persuasion, the whole structure of the play thus consisting of three parts), by Garvie, 216.

30. The text and English translation by R. C. Jebb, *Sophocles, the Plays and Fragments* IV, *The Philoctetes* (Cambridge, 1898) 103–105 (henceforth, Jebb, *Philoctetes*).

31. Garvie, 214.

32. G. Ronnet, *Sophocle, poète tragique* (Paris, 1969), 261 (henceforth, Ronnet).

33. Dio Chrysostom records that in Euripides' *Philoctetes*, produced in 431 B.C., Odysseus "complicated the plot and invented occasions for debates in the course of which he showed himself most resourceful and most proficient in combating the opposing arguments." (*Oration* 52.13, H. L. Crosby, *Dio Chrysostom* IV (London: Loeb Classical Library, 1946), 349. The date of Euripides' *Philoctetes* is given in *Medea*, hypothesis. For reconstruction, see W. M. Calder III, "A Reconstruction of Euripides, *Philoctetes*" in *Greek Numismatics and Archaeology: Essays in Honor of Margaret Thompson*, ed. O. Mørkholm and N. M. Waggoner (Belgium, 1979), 53–62 (henceforth, Calder, "Euripides, *Philoctetes*").

On Aeschylus' *Philoctetes* and date, see W. M. Calder III, "Aeschylus' *Philoctetes*," *GRBS* 11 (1970), 172ff. On Aeschylus' and Euripides' plays, Kieffer, 38ff.

34. Neoptolemus' struggle within himself has been thoroughly studied in W. Steidle, *Studien zum antiken Drama* (Munich, 1968), 169–92, especially 174, 179–81.

35. The theme of temptation and corruption of youth followed by the reassertion of natural virtues, discussed by M. H. Jameson, "Politics and the *Philoctetes*," *CP* 51 (1956), 219; P. W. Rose, "Sophocles' *Philoctetes* and the Teachings of the Sophists," *HSCP* 80 (1976), 102 (henceforth, Rose), Avery, 289.

36. Heracles' scene is brilliantly discussed by A. Spira, *Untersuchungen zum Deus ex Machina bei Sophokles und Euripides* (Kallmünz/Opf., 1960), 26–32.

37. On the importance of the first conclusion (1402–1408) for Philoctetes' heroism, see Robinson, 53.

38. Whitman, *Sophocles*, 187.

39. Neoptolemus' "sterling" character has deprived Odysseus of the scantiest sympathy he might have gained as a partisan of the Greek army, *e.g.*, Harsh, 409; C.P. Segal, "Philoctetes and the unperishable Piety," *Herm.* 105 (1977), 139 n.17; Rose, 88ff; G. Méautis, *Sophocles:essai sur le heros tragique*[2]

(Paris, 1957), 64 as "Mephistopheles."

40. Winnington-Ingram, *Sophocles,* 282.

41. In Euripides' *Philoctetes,* Odysseus makes a long speech in the safety and privacy of the prologue, presenting to the audience only, why "a task most hazardous and hard" has brought him to Lemnos: " 'tis difficult to find a thing so proud, so jealous of honour, as man is born to be. . . . This thirst for glory is what leads even me to bear unnumbered woes and live a life of toil beyond all other men, accepting ever fresh peril, fearing to mar the glory won by earlier achievements." (Paraphrased by Dio Chrysostom *Or.* 59.2) Once the deepest cravings of his fame-stricken heart is thus confided to the audience, they look upon the whole disgraceful work of the fetching of Philoctetes on that presupposition. Sophocles' picture of Odysseus adumbrated by the false merchant's speech is similarly vainglorious, but the unpleasant covetousness of the careerist is channelled through another, decreasing its impact on the audience. The ugliness of the publicity stunt and the desire for self-advancement is blurred by the semitransparent veil of sham.

Calder ("Euripides, *Philoctetes,*" 62) finds recollection of the Euripidean prologue in the tale of the false merchant of Sophocles. This *philotimia*-motif was presented in the Euripidean manner of polemic in *Phoenissae* produced in the same year as *Philoctetes. Cf.* J. de Romilly, "*Phoenician Women* of Euripides: Topicality in Greek Tragedy," *Bucknell Review,* vol.15, n.3 (Lewisburg, 1967), 116ff.

42. Ronnet, 262; Reinhardt, *Sophokles,* 196; Hinds, 179; Linforth, 134ff; Jebb, *Philoctetes* on 1004.

It is reported that in Euripides Odysseus took hold of the bow, with the help of Diomedes, during the sick man's fit, thus compelling him to yield. Likewise in Aeschylus, the bow was stolen during the paroxysm: Paus., 1.22.6; Robert, *Heldensage,* III.2. 1211 n.5. On Aeschylus, Tycho, 271; Kieffer, 39.

43. On the staging of Odysseus' brief appearance at 1293, see T. B. L. Webster, *Philoctetes* (Cambridge, 1970), 147 on line 1257.

44. *Oration* 52.16. Sophocles' Odysseus is often associated with contemporary sophists (Pohlenz, 334; Rose, 81ff). It may be worth noting that Euripides' play, according to Dio Chrysostom, was "most political, rhetorical, most useful to the readers" (*Oration* 52.11).

45. Quotation is from W. B. Stanford, *The Ulysses Theme* (Oxford, 1954, second edition revised, Blackwell, 1968), 40 (henceforth, Stanford, *Ulysses*).

46. Opportunism and the code of expediency are recommended as virtues of leading politicians in Thucydides: Themistocles (1.138) and Pericles (2.35–46) On Pericles' use of the word *eutrapelos,* see Knox, "*Ajax,*" 25.

47. The Athenian audience were presumably reminded of the moments in

earlier productions when the destitute Philoctetes departed for Troy, "persuaded by necessity" (Dio Chrysostom *Oration* 52.2). Dio does not explicitly state to which play this refers. Probably both to Aeschylus' and Euripides'. Euripides' Hypothesis (*P. Oxy.*2455 Fr.17.266 = Austin, *Nova Fragmenta Euripidea*, 100) described his Philoctetes as "compelled to follow to the ship."

48. Gellie, 132.

49. On the heroic ideal of Homer taken over by Sophocles, see Whitman, *Sophocles*, 59ff and 64; Knox, *Heroic Temper*, 50–53. Winnington-Ingram, *Sophocles*, 304 warns against overgeneralization but admits that the Sophoclean handling of the heroes bears the mark of "a certain—and, it seems, a remarkably stable—view of the world." *Cf.* R. M. Torrance, "Sophocles: Some Bearings," *HSCP* 69 (1965), 278 (henceforth, Torrance).

50. Stanford, *Ulysses,* 34. On *sophrosyne* in Sophocles, see H. North, *Sophrosyne: Self-Knowledge and Self-Restraint in Greek Literature* (Ithaca, New York, 1966) 50–68. *Cf.* Schmid-Stählin, I.2. 470n.16.

5. Some Additional Remarks

1. *Vita Eur.* 5.

2. For Sophocles' plays discussed in historical contexts, see among others: Ronnet and on *Ajax:* Brown, 1–28; *Antigone*: Calder, *"Antigone,"* 389–407; *Oedipus Rex*: Knox, *"Oedipus,"* 133–47; *Electra:* L. A. Post, "Sophocles, Strategy and the *Electra,"* CW 46 (1953), 150–53; *Philoctetes*: Jameson, 217–27; Calder, *"Apologia,"* 153–74; (*Oedipus Coloneus*: U. von Wilamowitz-Möllendorff *apud* Tycho, 318).

3. The "digression" (*Aj.* 1120–1123) on the respective merits of the archer and the hoplite has been noted, Brown, 17; *cf.* A. Plassart, "Les archers d'Athenes," *REG* 26 (1913), 197.

4. Plut., *Per.* 11–12.

5. M. Kubo, *Thucydides, History* (Japanese translation, Tokyo, 1974), vol. 1, 17.

6. *Eum.* 526ff. 692ff. *Cf.* Adkins, 76.

7. Arist., *Rhet.* 3.18.1419a.

8. For contemporary meanings of other words, *e.g., gennaios, kerdos, sympheronta*, see Calder, *"Apologia,"* 70–71; Rose, 68; Torrance, 287; Whitman, *Sophocles,* 179.

9. Sophocles as a repentant proboulos, P. Foucart, "Le poète Sophocle et l'oligarchi des Quatre Cents," *RevPhil* 17 (1893), 1–10; Calder, *"Apologia,"* 170–74.

10. Xenophon, *Mem.* 4.4.19ff Other references, Arist., *Pol.* 1.2.1252b 20; Pind., *Pyth.* 6.23ff; Eur., Fr.853N²; Isocr., 1.16. G. Glotz, *La solidarité de la famille dans le droit criminel en Grece* (Paris, 1904) 31ff; *cf.* G. Thomson (ed.), *The Oresteia of Aeschylus* (Cambridge, 1938), I.51ff, II.269ff, 362ff.

The idea of complete submission to the gods' behest may be seen in Fr.247R.

11. In Aeschylus' *Eumenides* (660), Apollo says that a father is more important than a mother. A similar notion is stressed or taken for granted in Ajax's consideration for Telamon and Eurysaces, Creon's speech (*Ant.* 162–91, 666–76), Heracles' will (*Trach.* 1177–1178, *cf.* 1244), and the speech of Archidamas (Thuc., 1.80–85 (especially 84.3–4), 2.11).

12. On divination and the Athenians of the fifth century B.C. see, *e.g.*, Plut, *Per.* 6; Thuc., 7.50, 8.1 and the constant jokes in comedy; A. Powell, "Thucydides and Divination," *BICS* 26 (1979), 45–50.

13. Of Draco's laws (*ca.* 621 B.C.) those that dealt with homicide survived Solon's repeal or revision (*ca.* 593 B.C.). His originality lies in the distinction he made between wilful murders and unpunishable ones. See on unintentional homicide: D. M. MacDowell, *Athenian homicide law in the age of the orators* (Manchester, 1963), 58–60; "Unintentional Homicide in the *Hippolytos*," *Rh. Mus.* 111 (1968), 156–58.

14. *Cf. supra* chapter 3, p. 00.

15. W. K. C. Guthrie, *Orpheus and Greek Religion*² (London, 1952), 114.

16. Apollod., *Bibl.* 3.14.8; Ov., *Met.* 6.424.

17. Thuc., 2.101; *cf.* 6.90, 7.29 and the Triballian of Ar., *Aves.*

18. *Cf.* The satire in Ar., *Ach.* (425 B.C.), 134ff; Polymestor in Eur., *Hec.* 424 B.C.?); *Erechtheus* (422 B.C.). *Cf.* Goosens 295–96.

19. Winnington-Ingram, *Sophocles,* 75ff.

20. R. P. Winnington-Ingram, *BICS* 16 (1969), 45ff; C. Segal, "Sophocles' *Trachiniae*: Myth, Poetry and Heroic Values," *YCS* 25 (1977), 119–23; C. E. Sorum, "Monsters and the Family: the Exodus of Sophocles' *Trachiniae*," *GRBS* 19 (1978), 64.

21. Winnington-Ingram, *Sophocles,* 83.

22. Note how similar Deianeira's reflections before death (721–22) are to Ajax's (479).

23. On the legend before Attic tragedy, see Barrett, *Hippolytus,* 6–10.

24. Barrett, *Hippolytus,* 12 and note 1. It is assumed that the *katabasis* motif (a descent to *Hades,* the world of the dead) of Theseus was introduced into drama by Sophocles: L. Meridier, *Mélanges G. Glotz* (Paris, 1932), II.591ff; H. Weil, *Sept tragedies d'Euripide* (Paris, 1868), 6; but see H. Herter, "Theseus der Athener," *Rh. Mus.,* 88 (1939) and 89 (1940).

25. On the attribution of Frr.679R, 680R, and 684R to Phaedra, see Barrett, *Hippolytus*, 12 and n.1.

26. Webster, *Monuments*, 151: "Classical Background to Racine's Phèdre," 303–304.

27. Fr.682R sounds like a gnomic phrase of popular philosophy. But the last line, "each one sepaks of what he himself has met and undergone," suggests that it is spoken by Theseus. who has seen what Phaedra's love for Hippolytus has led to. If so, the inconsiderate nature of the remark suggests a gulf between Theseus and Phaedra similar to that between Heracles and Deianeira.

28. Webster, *Euripides*, 75.

29. Hence the title *Hippolytus Kalyptomenos*.

30. Hypothesis to *Second Hippolytus*.

31. Aristotle says that Sophocles professed to create his dramatic figures as human beings ought to be, while Euripides depicted them as they were (Arist., *Poet.* 25.1460b). Perhaps Phaedra was one of the plays that were in Sophocles' mind when he made this remark.

32. On *eukleia* of Phaedra in *Second Hippolytus*, see H. Strohm, *Euripides* (Munich, 1957), 104 n.1.

33. Hypothesis to *Second Hippolytus*.

34. Kitto (chapter 2, n.54) has elucidated how Sophoclean tragedy unfolds on dual planes, human and divine, and further pointed out the close interplay between human and divine dramas. Fr.589R is perfectly understandable in that context.

35. By and large, all sorts of mental and physical experiences could be attributed to the interventions of some external power in Homer. Homeric heroes could impute everything to the gods (*e.g.*, *Il.* 16.843ff, 19.86ff. *cf.* Nilsson 122ff). According to Snell, who discussed free will (*Entdeckung*, 153 and *Scenes*, 1–22), Achilles merely knew it to be his own fate to die a young man in a blaze of glory or to live a long and obscure life. (*Cf.* A. Lesky, "Göttliche und menschliche Motivation im homerischen Epos," *Sitzungsberichte der Heidelberger Akademie der Wissenschaften phil-his. Klasse*, 1961, 100) In Snell's interpretation, Aeschylean heroes are recognized to be making personal decisions and thus assuming responsibility with the future course of action. Still in Aeschylus a sense of divine providence, more often of divine infatuation (*ate*), overhangs human moral behaviour.

36. Reinhardt, *Sophokles*, 20, 22; J. Jones, *On Aristotle and Greek Tragedy* (Oxford, 1962), 11–20, 82, 90.

Index Locorum

Accius, Fr.87W:135; Fr.88–89W:135; Fr93–94W:135; Frr.272–73W:22, 23, 24, 27, 34, 44, 134, 136; Fr.274W:22, 34, 136; Fr.275W:22, 23, 24, 27, 33, 34, 44, 136; Fr.276W:22, 23, 35; Fr.277–79W:22, 23, 27, 28, 29, 32, 34, 35, 38, 43, 48, 136; Fr.280W:22, 30, 35, 136; Fr.281W:22, 23, 24, 26, 28, 30, 36, 44, 137; Frr.282–83W:22, 36; Frr.284–85W:23, 27, 29, 33, 38, 136; Fr.286W:23, 30, 35, 136; Fr.287W:23, 38, 39, 137; Fr.288W:23, 39, 137; Fr.289W:23, 29, 34, 38, 39, 136, 137; Fr.290W:23, 41, 137; Frr.291–93W:23, 41, 134; Fr.294W:23, 42; Fr.326W:39, 137; Frr.639–42W:69, 79, 80; Frr.643–44W:61, 70; Frr.645–46W:65; Fr.647W:66, 67, 79, 144; Frr.648–49W:68; Fr.650W:70; Fr.651W:70; Frr.652–53W:60, 69; Fr.654W:71, 81; Fr.655W:64; Frr. Inc. Inc. Trag. (Accius?), 25–26, 27–28:136
Achilles Tatius, 5.3.5:144; 5.5:142, 143
Aelianus, *Var. Hist.*, 12.20:57
Aeschylus,
  Ag., 463ff:129, 792ff:129, 919:55, 958ff:6, 1146:141
Cho., 1050ff.:47
Eum., 1ff:47, 526ff:153, 660ff:154, 692ff:153
Pers., 1–154:7, 241:55, 400:55, 742ff:6, 743:7, 808:6, 827ff:6, 897:148
Prom., 88ff:138
Sept., 463:55, 653–76:138, 745ff:6, 769ff:129
Supp., 60–67:141; 1001ff:6; Fr.212M (= Ar. *Ran.*911–24):129; Fr.243aM (= *Vita Aesch.*6):129; Fr.283M:7, 129; Fr.285M:132; Fr.304M:148; Fr.305M:148; Fr.368M:139
Vita Aesch., 6:129, 8–9:140, 15:147
Alcman, Fr.1 16–18:128
Antiphanes Fr.191 II90K, (= Athen. 6.223):31, 40, 134
Apollodorus
  Bibl., 3.5.6:129, 142; 3.6.1:20; 3.7.2ff.:20, 27, 43, 44; 3.14.8:64, 67, 142, 143, 154
  Epit., 5.22:131, 6.8:148, 6.20–22:131
  Schol. to Apollonius Rhodius, 3.1040:53, 4.223:53
Archilochus, Fr.7. 7–9:128, Fr.58:128, Fr.74:128,
Aristophanes
  Ach., 134ff:154, 377–82:140
  Av., 99:61, 100:74, 280:141, 281:57, 1346–1368:114
  Lys., 563:71, 81, 144

157

Homerus
  Il., 2.594–600:127, 2.867:54,
    3.1ff.:141, 4.429–36:141,
    5.407ff.:4, 6.138ff.:4,
    16.843ff.:155,17.71:128,
    19.86ff.:155, 19.258–65:131,
    24.525-33:128
  Od., 1.1–4:87, 3.135:11, 3.145:11,
    4.181ff:128, 4.502:11,
    5.108ff:11, 5.118ff:128,
    8.565ff:128,11.422:131,
    13.173ff:128, 13.287ff:4,
    15.248:134,19.518:141,
    19.523:49, 23.210ff:128
  Schol. to Homerus *Il*.1.37:131;
    2.595:127; A 24.602:129, 142;
    V. *Od*.11.326:20
Horatius, *Ars P*.187:62
Hyginus, *Fab.*, 8:25, 9.2–4:129,
    9.3:129, 73:20

Inscriptiones Graecae, *IG* I²202 1.36:140,
    (Marm. Par.)12(5) 444:52
Isocrates, *Ep*.1.16:154

Lactantius on Statius *Theb.*, 6.117:129
Libanius
  Narr., 4.1103:142, 4.1103 I17–18:67
  Refutat., 8.128ff:131
Lucianus, *De Salt*.46:11, 131
Lycophron, 348ff.:131

Macrobius, *Sat*.5.18.8:53

Nonnus
  Dion.4.321:142, 12.75:142

Ovidius
  Met.6.165–203:130; 6.289:129;
    6.422–676:59; 6.424:154;
    6.459–60:146; 6.527–28:79;
    6.563–66:78; 6.566–70:66;
    6.571:66; 6.572ff.:66; 6.577:67;
    6.580:61; 6.581–86:61;

6.582–83:67; 6.587:66, 67, 80;
    6.590:79; 6.601ff.:68;
    6.611ff.:69; 6.620:62;
    6.642ff.:69; 6.647ff.:70;
    6.648:81; 6.650:70, 71;
    6.653:81; 6.658–60:71;
    7.159–296:130
Oxyrhychus Papyri
  P. Oxy., 2256 fr.3 ("Danaid" pa-
    pyrus):146
  P. Oxy., 2455 fr.17.266 (Eur. *Phil.*
    Hypothesis):153
  P. Oxy., 2805, see Sophocles
  P. Oxy., 3013 (*Tereus*
    Hypothesis):58ff, 78, 142
  P. Oxy., 3151, see Sophocles

Paroemiographi Graeci
  App.Prov., 3.35(Leutsch/Schneidewin
    I 423) (= Fr.201hR):27, 138
  Zenobius, 3.14 (Leutsch/Schneidewin
    I 61):142
Pausanias, 1.15.2:131, 1.22.6:152,
    1.34.3:138,3.15.8:135,
    5.17.7:135, 9.5.5:135, 9.5.15:29,
    9.8.6:138, 9.9.4:138, 9.30.2:10,
    10.4.9:142, 10.30.8:130,
    10.31.2:131
Philodemus, *De Mus*.1.30Kemk:40
Phrynichus Fr.31K:140
Pindar
  Nem.4.46:148, 8.25–34:147
  Pyth.6.23ff:154, 8.61–80:128
Plutarchus
  Anat.17.760:9
  An seni 785B:140
  De aud. poet.35E:31
  De Herod. Malign.857A:141
  Nic.15:140
  Per.6:154, 8:140, 11–12:153
Pollux, *Onom*.4.141:127
Proclus
  from *Cypria* (= E.G.F.18):147,
    (=E.G.F.19):148